SPIEGEL & GRAU

ALSO BY SUZE ORMAN

Women & Money

The Money Book for the Young, Fabulous & Broke

The Laws of Money, The Lessons of Life

The Road to Wealth

The Courage to Be Rich

Suze Orman's Financial Guidebook

The 9 Steps to Financial Freedom

You've Earned It, Don't Lose It

SUZE ORMAN'S

2009 ACTION PLAN

SPIEGEL & GRAU

New York

2009

This book is designed to provide accurate and authoritative information about personal finances. Neither the author nor the publisher is engaged in rendering legal, accounting, or other professional services by publishing this book. If any such assistance is required, the services of a qualified financial professional should be sought. The author and publisher will not be responsible for any liability, loss, or risk incurred as a result of the use and application of any of the information contained in this book.

While the author has made every effort to provide accurate telephone numbers and Internet addresses at the time of publication, neither the publisher nor the author assumes any responsibility for errors or for changes that occur after publication.

A Certified Financial Planner® is a federally registered mark owned by the Certified Financial Planner Board of Standards, Inc.

Published in the United States by Spiegel & Grau, an imprint of The Doubleday Publishing Group, a division of Random House, Inc., New York
www.spiegelandgrau.com

SPIEGEL & GRAU is a trademark of Random House, Inc.

Book design by Chris Welch

Cataloging-in-Publication Data is on file with
the Library of Congress

ISBN 978-0-385-53093-4

PRINTED IN THE UNITED STATES OF AMERICA

1 3 5 7 9 8 6 4 2

First Edition

CONTENTS

SUZE ORMAN'S

2009 ACTION PLAN

1

2009: The New Reality

I bet you are scared. Angry, too. And confused. These are absolutely rational and appropriate responses to the global credit crisis that erupted in 2008 and continues to send tremors through every household in America. And I do mean every household. No matter how conscientious you have been with managing your money, the events of 2008 have battered us all.

The one in 10 homeowners who are at risk of facing foreclosure on their homes are obviously scared, but so too are the 9 out of 10 homeowners who can afford their mortgage but are watching plummeting home values jeopardize their financial security.

It's not just the overreaching Wall Street firms who are paying the price for those risky investments. Every U.S. taxpayer is now on the hook for a massive bailout—a bailout engineered by the same players in the federal government that had turned their back on regulating the very practices at the root of today's financial crisis. Angry? You should be.

But wait—it gets worse: The colossal miscalculations on Wall Street have contributed to a massive decline in the value of your 401(k) and IRA. Years of diligent saving have been wiped out, and you are afraid that your retirement accounts will never fully recover.

Early predictions that the fallout in the consumer credit markets would be limited to subprime lending to borrowers with low credit scores proved terribly wrong. The truth is that credit lines are being reeled in and home equity lines of credit are being rescinded across the board as banks worry that their clients—even those with solid payment histories—won't be able to keep up with the bills if the current crisis turns into a deep recession. A sparkling FICO credit score is no longer a guarantee that you will land a mortgage or car loan with decent terms. Right now lenders are more interested in keeping any available cash on their books, rather than out on loan.

There is also a growing sense that repercussions from the credit crisis will turn what might have been a moderate economic slowdown in 2009 into an especially deep recession. If that scenario plays out, businesses will likely announce more and bigger layoffs than we saw in 2008, when unemployment rose from 4.9% to 6.5% at the end of October. In 2009, your job may be on the line as your employer, or your own business, struggles with the fallout from the credit crisis.

That's a daunting platter of problems to contend with. Did I say daunting? What I meant was overwhelming.

As the economic outlook grew more troubling, I came to the realization that I had to write this book and get it published quickly. You want to do what's right, but it's no longer clear what right is anymore. Or perhaps you are someone who always figured you had time to deal with the money issues in your life *later.* The credit crisis has woken you up; later is now—but where do you start?

This book's title is a promise. This is my Action Plan for every important financial move you need to make in 2009. Follow the advice here and you will know exactly what you need to do to adapt to the new post-meltdown reality. Just as important, you will know what *not* to do. In times of great stress, it is natural to react by making decisions and taking actions that bring instant relief. When it comes to financial matters, often the decisions that calm us amid tumult are actions that can imperil our long-term security. In the pages that follow, I will tell you when to act and when to leave it be—which will, in some cases, require a little bit of faith and nerves of steel, but I promise I will never steer you wrong or put your dreams of a secure future in peril. You can count on me.

Accent on *Action*

I want to be very clear about something that is central to my Action Plan: You must commit to actually taking action. This is not a book to be read and pondered. Or filed away under "Nice to know; I'll get to it." If you care about financial security for yourself and your family, if you want to do everything in your power to protect yourself and your future, you will not get there with wishful thinking or procrastination. You cannot sit this one out, hoping that the storm will pass and everything will be just fine. If you do nothing, I am sorry to say you may be in even deeper trouble in 2010. The fact is, the new reality requires new strategies. They will not necessarily be wholesale changes in every aspect of your financial life, but tactical actions to make sure you do not let the credit crisis knock you off course.

Some of the most crucial actions require pushing yourself to stay committed to all the smart moves you have already made but may now be questioning. I know many of you are thinking there is no point in continuing to invest for retirement as long as the markets are down. Big, big mistake. Now is an incredibly smart time to invest for retirement, because the markets are down—

assuming, of course, you have at least 10 years until you will need that money. Same goes for your 529 college savings plan for a young child.

There is to be no curling up in a fetal position on the couch in 2009 hoping that when you emerge the crisis will have passed. No assuming that there is a government bailout or Wall Street rally right around the corner that will fix everything for you without any effort on your part. You will have to get off the couch and take control of your financial life in 2009. Make that commitment this year and you will build a solid financial foundation that you can stand on when everything around you is crumbling and that you can build on when the good times return.

We Will Survive

As we continue to claw our way out of the credit crisis while contending with an economic recession, I need you to be able to see the big picture: Though these are rocky times, our economy will be fine. Our markets will recover. We will all survive. That said, I want to be very clear: The recovery is not going to be quick or easy.

Our economy is like a patient who was rushed to the hospital in critical condition. After months of aggressive intervention (by the Federal Reserve, the Department of Treasury, and Congress), the patient is still in the Intensive Care Unit, but the prognosis is that eventually there will be a full recovery. In time, the patient will move into a rehabilitation facility and start to get back on his or her feet. Before too long, the patient will be stable enough to go home, though it might be years before he or she is back to full health.

When exactly will that be? That's impossible to say with any certainty. My sense is that we could be in for a long, slow period of recovery and it will be 2014 or 2015 before the economy is back in robust good health. Between now and then, we could see parts of our economy get better faster than others, and certainly some regions will start their housing rebound before others. I also expect there could be large market rallies throughout a rocky recovery. It is also important to understand that the stock market is very different than the economy. Just because the market rallies, it doesn't mean the economy is healthy. But in terms of when we will see a lasting and consistent return to growth, well, I wouldn't be surprised if that takes five years or more.

So if we're not going to see a quick turnaround of the economy in 2009, why am I insisting that you take action? Precisely because we are in for tough times. You need to protect what you have. Protect your family. And protect your chances of still reaching your long-term goals. Let's face it, in the past you didn't really have to work too hard at building financial security. You plowed money into your 401(k) and IRA in the 1990s and you watched the market post an annualized gain of 18%. At that rate, you figured early retirement was a distinct possibility. Then, in 2000, the real estate bubble began and you got used to annual price gains of 10% or more. It was easy to feel like you had it made.

And yet here we are. The major stock market benchmark indexes have fallen back to where they were in 1998. Home values, on average, have already slid back to their 2004 levels, and I expect we have more downside to get through before real estate stabilizes. My point is, you just can't show up and expect easy market gains to get you where you want to go. The days of easy money are long gone.

But, my friends, haven't I always said that when it comes to your money, it's not about doing what's easy—it's about doing what's right? The plan in this book is going to help you do what's right. You can read this book cover to cover, go directly to the topic that worries you the most, or skip around as you see fit. No matter how you approach it, the goal is for you to make the right moves in 2009 to alleviate the stress, fear, and anger you're feeling and replace it with the secure sense that you have done what it takes to protect yourself, the money you have worked so hard for, and the ones you love.

2

A Brief History of How We Got Here

By now you probably have some sense that back in 2007 the financial crisis began because a sizable number of homeowners started to fall behind on their mortgage payments. But you may be wondering how it is that a relatively small portion of people who failed to make their mortgage payments could bring the global economy to its knees.

The short answer, in my opinion, is greed. Too many people were more interested in making a quick buck than making sound financial decisions. Mortgage lenders stopped caring whether borrowers were actually qualified to buy a home and gave out loans to practically anyone who applied. Wall Street banks and hedge funds stoked the lenders to give out those loans so they could then turn around and make tons of money off of them with newfangled investing schemes. And while some borrowers were indeed too confused or clueless to understand their mortgages, others knew exactly what they were doing and didn't care that they were buying homes they couldn't afford. Plenty of greed to go around.

It wasn't always this way. Not all that long ago, if you wanted to get a mortgage you showed up at the bank armed with a few years of tax records and pay stubs to verify your income, as well as proof that you had enough savings to make a down payment of 20%. The lender then took time to review your finances carefully, making sure there was indeed plenty of income to comfortably cover the mortgage, property tax, and insurance, and that you were not overly burdened with other debt payments. The only choice you had was a 15-year fixed-rate mortgage or a 30-year fixed-rate mortgage. There was no guesswork about what would happen to your interest rate in the future, no such thing as an adjustable-rate mortgage (ARM); if a lender agreed to give you a mortgage, you both knew what your payments would be for the life of that loan. If the loan was approved, the bank was betting that you would have the ability to repay it on time for the duration of the mortgage. If a lender didn't think you were likely to keep paying the mortgage for 30 years (or until you sold the home), you were denied the mortgage. It was that simple. This protected the bank, and it protected the borrower from taking debt they could not afford.

The relationship between the bank and the borrower began its seismic shift in the early 1980s. This is where Fannie Mae and Freddie Mac come into our story. Fannie was created in 1938 and Freddie followed in 1970; both were government-sponsored enterprises (GSEs)—they weren't full-blown federal agencies, but they had the aura of being government-backed. Both GSEs had a straightforward mandate: to increase the amount of money available for mortgages. They did this by buying mortgages from lenders so the lenders would then have more money to lend. Fannie and Freddie packaged loans that they held in their own portfolios, as well as guaranteeing mortgages that Wall Street could then package and sell to investors. This entire process is what spurred homebuying, because the lenders had more money to lend to potential homebuyers, which allowed more and more people to buy homes.

At this point it became increasingly likely that the original lender would not hold on to the mortgage, but would instead sell it to a loan packager such as Fannie or Freddie (or their less-well-known cousin, Ginnie Mae) and Wall Street firms. Still, mortgage-backed securities had a very good reputation—they were new income products that were backed by solid mortgages. Lenders were still careful to make loans only to borrowers who could meet their high standards. It is important to note that the business of packaging mortgages—what's known as securitization—in itself is not bad. It is, in fact, an important and positive innovation for financial markets. The problem began around the beginning of the twenty-first century, when Wall Street and greedy lenders cooked up a scheme that took a good idea and turned it into a toxic time bomb, with a major assist from the Federal Reserve.

Once the technology stock bubble began to deflate in early 2000, Federal Reserve chairman Alan Greenspan attempted to keep the economy from slipping into a severe recession by slashing the Federal Funds Rate. From 2000 to 2004, the rate fell from above 6% to 1%. In such a low-rate environment, Wall Street set out to create an investment that was perceived to be safe and would offer higher yields than basic bank CDs and money markets were offering. The too-smart-for-our-own-good minds of the financial sector set their sights on the quiet and somewhat staid world of mortgage-backed securities. Rather than only packaging plain-vanilla mortgages that had been taken out by well-qualified borrowers, they realized there was a lot more money to be made by expanding the market to include mortgages that had been made to people who were not well qualified. Mortgages made to people without good credit were known as subprime mortgages. Wall

Street insisted it had come up with a way to package subprime mortgages with solid mortgages that would give investors a higher yield, but with no added risk. Wall Street bundled the prime and subprime mortgages together in one investment, called a Credit Default Obligation (CDO). Mortgage-backed CDOs were supposed to be low-risk because of how they pooled and divided the risk of the underlying mortgages.

But Wall Street wasn't done with its great mortgage-backed money grab. It also started churning out massive amounts of Credit Default Swaps (CDS) tied to mortgages. The CDS were insurance that promised investors in mortgage-backed securities that they would be paid even if an underlying investment (your mortgage) went into default. Wall Street was also able to make massive bets on mortgages using CDS.

Now I need to take a quick detour and mention another important player in this crisis: leverage. Not only was Wall Street allowed to create these credit default swaps and other so-called safe investments, they also were allowed to leverage those investments to create more and more money for themselves. When you leverage, you are borrowing money in order to have more money to invest. Here's an example: Say you have $1 of your own, but someone gives you $2 so you have $3 to invest. If your investment pans out, you simply return the $2 with interest, but you get to keep all the profits from your $3 investment. That's a lot more profit than if you had just invested $1. Wall Street has used leverage for years, but during this mortgage craziness, it talked federal regulators into allowing it to borrow up to $30 or more for every dollar it actually owned. And Wall Street firms leveraged themselves to the hilt to make big bets on mortgage-backed securities and all sorts of schemes, including credit default swaps.

With their ingenious moneymaking scheme in place, the only remaining obstacle for Wall Street and the lenders was how to ramp up the numbers of subprime borrowers. This is when we started seeing an array of unconventional mortgages, such as interest-only mortgages, negative-amortization mortgages, payment-option ARMs, and 1-year ARMs with artificially low initial payments. (Interest-only mortgages and payment-option mortgages, two of the riskiest and insane types of ARMs, grew from 2% of the mortgage market in 2003 to 20% in 2005.) And all you needed to qualify was a heartbeat. No down payment? No problem. Nor did borrowers need to cough up tax returns or pay stubs to verify their income. That was so twentieth century; this was the new world where NINJA loans ruled. No Income, No Job, No Assets. No problem, you still qualify!

Mortgage lenders were happy to make these risky loans, because they knew it wouldn't be their problem if the borrower eventually ran into trouble keeping up with the payments. Why? Because these loans would quickly be sold off to investors, and the investors were happy to do the deal because they were being told that they had "insurance" against mortgage defaults from the credit default swaps. Oh, happy days.

Lenders couldn't lend money fast enough to satisfy the appetite of Wall Street investors and borrowers were encouraged to take out the biggest mortgage possible. Everyone wanted their piece of the American Dream as home values skyrocketed.

But the cracks began to appear in late 2006 and early 2007. Borrowers who had taken out an adjustable-rate mortgage a few years earlier faced their first rate adjustment. Many were shocked by new payments that were far beyond what they could afford. Refinancing into a more affordable mortgage wasn't an option for many people, because the Federal Reserve at that time had now been raising the Federal Funds Rate, which by mid-2006 was above 5%. This meant that adjustable-rate mortgages—many of which are affected by changes in the Federal Funds Rate—would be more expensive now that the rate was so much higher. At the same time, real estate values started to stagnate in many areas, and many ARM borrowers simply didn't have enough equity built up in their homes to be able to refinance, no matter what the interest rate. Remember, too, that many people were able to buy a home for no money down so they never had equity to begin with.

By 2007, there were suddenly a whole lot of homeowners who couldn't afford their mortgages, couldn't refinance, and couldn't sell at a price that would cover their mortgage because real estate prices had begun to slide. And lenders were in no mood to strike any deals. That's when the foreclosure rate started to rise. Far from being a problem confined to subprime borrowers in over their heads, foreclosures soon sent home values plummeting everywhere. If your neighbor's home was in foreclosure, that was bad news for you too. Since the 2006 peak, home values have dropped more than 20% on average, and twice as much in some markets that were once considered to be among the hottest. Many people owe more on their homes than what they could sell them for today. In fact, as I write this an estimated one in six homeowners have a mortgage that exceeds the value of their home in today's market—a situation that is known as being under water.

As foreclosures began to spread—Moody's Economy.com estimates nearly 2.5 million homes were lost in 2007 and 2008 and another 3.5 million could be lost in 2009 and 2010—the damage hit Wall Street. This is where leverage reenters the picture. Remember all that borrowing I mentioned earlier? Well, a lot of it was used to invest in all sorts of mortgage-related securities. When those investments began to fall apart because so many of the underlying mortgages that were the basis of those bets were now in foreclosure, investors faced the ugly downside of leverage: They had borrowed a lot of money and now had no money to pay it back. At 30:1 leverage, a Wall Street player could make bets with a value of $300 million even if it had just $10 million of its own money backing that bet. If the bet didn't pay off, the bank or hedge fund had no way to make good on the $300 million. And the supposed "insurance" from CDS was just an empty promise. No one had the money to make good on those deals.

To review: We had lenders making loans that borrowers couldn't afford, borrowers happy to get a mortgage they couldn't afford, and Wall Street, egging on lenders and borrowers, telling us that it was all okay because they insisted they had a brilliant way to insulate investors (and their own trading operations) against the risk in making highly leveraged bets, because in the unlikely event borrowers actually fell into trouble, the credit default swaps would save the day.

That, of course, is a very basic explanation, and there are many, many other elements that came into play. But I want to cut to the real issue here: *We are in trouble today because everyone was happy to lie, or happy to believe lies that any sane person could see right through.*

I cannot overstate my wrath at mortgage lenders that pushed toxic loans on borrowers, knowing there was little chance they could honestly afford those loans. While some borrowers were simply too confused to understand what they were getting into, I cannot absolve those who chose to drink the Kool-Aid that they could buy a $350,000 house on an income that could realistically pay for only a $150,000 one. Nor do I have much patience for borrowers who tell me the problem is that real estate prices stopped going up, so they got stuck without enough equity to refinance or sell. Buying a house based on the expectation that price gains were a given and would continue to rise at an annual pace that was double and triple the historical norm is not just foolish, it's greedy! Borrowers chose to believe what they wanted to believe.

And don't get me started on the levels of dishonesty perpetrated by the banks and hedge funds that came up with this can't-miss scheme and the government policy that did little to provide the regulation that might prevent a meltdown. Or the fact that Fannie Mae and Freddie Mac also got in on the act and lowered their underwriting standards so they could participate in the booming loan market.

It was a wild, drunken party of dishonesty and greed on a national scale.

The Honest Way Out

While the mortgage crisis is the most vivid example of how dishonesty and greed leads to financial destruction, it is by no means the only example. If you have a credit card balance that will remain unpaid at the end of this month, you are participating in your own brand of dishonesty because you are living beyond your means. If you have no emergency savings fund, you are not being honest about considering and preparing for all the possibilities life may throw at you. Leasing a car rather than buying a car that is affordably financed with a standard three-year loan is, in my opinion, a form of financial deception. Thinking you didn't need to invest in your 401(k) or IRA because you could count on steep appreciation in your home to fund a comfortable retirement is irresponsible, wishful thinking. If you keep spending like crazy on the kids because, well, they expect you to, even though you have unpaid bills, that's a huge slice of dishonesty. If you are tapping your home equity to pay for vacations you can't really afford, you are cheating yourself out of financial security.

The lies need to stop. Just think about where all this dishonesty leaves you. In credit card debt. Without a savings safety net if something goes wrong. With no security.

You know that I have never thought this behavior made any sense. Those of you who have been watching *The Suze Orman Show* on CNBC, or following my advice elsewhere, know that I have forever advised against these acts of dishonesty. I find it incredibly gratifying to have helped so many of you change course. But I also know there are many more people who have yet to mend their ways or figured they had time to turn over a new leaf. Well, your time is up. If you don't get your act together in 2009, you will be in more trouble than you can imagine.

The reality you need to grasp is that the rules have changed. Credit card companies once giddy to help you pour on debt are now going to penalize you harshly if you are in debt or look like you might overload soon. A loan, be it a mortgage, car loan, or student loan, is much harder (and more expensive) to come by now. Nor can you rely on a credit line or HELOC in the event you are laid off in 2009 and need cash to keep your household running; the odds are that if you tap either credit source you will trigger a series of unintended consequences that can put you in even worse financial shape.

There is a way out: Honesty. With yourself. With your partner. With your children. If you are ready to face up to what you can honestly afford, if you are willing to live within your means, not within your dreams, you can turn this around. If you are ready to commit to an action plan that makes sure there is enough money left over at the end of the month to pay every bill and save money too, you are on your way to living a life of financial security.

But you have to be willing to get honest about every facet of your financial life.

My 2009 Action Plan gives you every honest answer you will need to navigate the treacherous financial situation we face today, but even more important, it will put you and your family on the path to safety and security, this year and every year.

3

ACTION PLAN

Credit

The New Reality

The banking industry is running scared. They think you won't be able to keep up with your credit card payments in 2009 as the nation continues to work its way through this economic meltdown. Of course, that's a justifiable concern whenever the economy slows down, jobs are lost, and unemployment rises. But what's different in 2009 is that banks are already reeling from the mortgage-default crisis that has triggered bank failures and shotgun marriages between weak banks and less-weak banks. Banks aren't exactly in great shape these days and they are painfully aware of a Category 3 hurricane about to bear down on them: National credit card debt is at a staggering $970 billion, 50% higher than when the last economic slowdown hit in 2000. That's what happens in an era of "easy" money where banks irresponsibly hand out multiple credit cards to anyone with a pulse, regardless of income, and consumers are all too eager to play along.

The game, however, is up, my friends. Credit card companies have reversed course. They are now looking for ways to lend less money, especially on accounts they deem risky: consumers with high unpaid balances and poor FICO credit scores. Reducing credit card limits, closing down accounts with no warning, and abruptly increasing interest rates are just some of the aggressive tactics the card companies are implementing right now to shore up their business. That means serious repercussions for you throughout 2009. Your FICO score may drop—not because you changed your financial behavior, but because the credit card companies changed the rules on you.

The best way to insulate yourself is to get out of credit card debt once and for all. If you pay off your balance, you don't have to worry about the interest rate on your card. If you pay off your balance, you are less likely to have your credit card limit reduced; and even if it is reduced, it will not have a negative impact on your FICO score.

If you pay off your credit card balance, you can focus on building an emergency savings fund. That's especially important in 2009. The days of using your credit card as a de facto emergency fund are over. If you tap too much of your credit card line, it is likely you will see the line reduced, your interest rate rise, and, yes, potentially have your card closed down—and there goes your FICO score. Unpaid balances in 2009 will put you in the middle of a vicious cycle. You must get out of card debt now. It is the number one action to take in 2009.

What you must do in 2009

- Make it a priority to pay off your credit card balances.
- Read every statement and all correspondence from your credit card company to make sure you are aware of any changes to your account, such as skyrocketing interest rates.
- Work to get your FICO credit score above 720.
- Be very careful where you turn to for help with credit card debt. Debt consolidators are often a very bad deal. The National Foundation for Credit Counseling is a smarter choice.
- Resist the temptation to use retirement savings or a home equity line of credit to pay off credit card debt.

Your 2009 Action Plan: Credit

SITUATION: You always pay the minimum amount due on your credit card bill and are never late, but your credit card limit was just reduced.

ACTION: Paying the minimum in 2009 is not good enough. Credit card companies are anticipating that as the recession plays out, consumers will be hard-pressed to keep up with their bills. So even if you have paid on time in the past, they are worried about what will happen in the future. And the fact that you pay just the minimum is a huge warning signal to your credit card company. It's a tip-off that you may already be on shaky ground.

Paying just the monthly minimum due signifies to a credit card company that you may fall behind on payments in a severe recession and that you are also more likely to let your balance grow if you hit hard times. And that's the last thing they want in 2009. To keep you from doing just that, they cut your credit limit.

SITUATION: You are worried that a lower credit limit will hurt your FICO credit score.

ACTION: Pay off your balance every month and your FICO credit score will not be affected. Your FICO credit score is based on a series of calculations that measure how good a credit risk you are. One of the biggest factors in your credit score—accounting for about 30% of your score—is how much debt you have. There are a few ways that this specific calculation is done, but one of the chief ways it's determined is the debt-to-available-credit ratio. Debt is how much money you owe on all your credit cards. Available credit is the sum of all the credit lines that have been extended to you. The higher your debt, the worse it is for your FICO score. And your debt-to-credit ratio will look much worse if your credit limit is cut.

Let's say you have only one credit card that has a $2,000 balance on it. Last year your credit limit on that card was $10,000. So your debt-to-credit ratio was 20% ($2,000 is 20% of $10,000). Now you find out that your credit card company has reduced your credit line to $5,000. That means your ratio shoots up to 40% ($2,000 is 40% of $5,000). That will indeed have a negative impact on your FICO score.

The only way to keep your FICO score unaffected by a credit-limit reduction is to get out of credit card debt and pay off your bills in full each month.

SITUATION: The credit card company canceled your account. Do you still have to pay the remaining balance?

ACTION: Of course you do! When your account is canceled, it is because the credit card company has labeled you a high-risk cardholder. What is being canceled is your ability to use that card in the future. But you are still responsible for every penny of your existing balance.

SITUATION: Your credit card has been canceled and you are worried it will hurt your FICO score.

ACTION: Focus on getting the balance paid off; the lower the balance, the less it will damage your FICO score if your card is canceled.

There are two issues that come up when a card is canceled: how it affects your debt-to-credit-limit ratio and what happens to the interest rate on your unpaid balance. In most cases, when a card that has a balance on it has been revoked or canceled, the credit card company will immediately raise your interest rate to about 30%. When this happens, if you continue to pay only the minimum monthly payment, you may never get out of debt on that card.

SITUATION: You thought the interest rate on your credit card was fixed at 5%, but it just shot up to 30%!

ACTION: There is no such thing as a permanent fixed interest rate on your credit card. The rate is fixed only until the credit card issuer decides it isn't. It's a marketing ploy. And credit card companies have all sorts of reasons (embedded in the agreement you accepted when you opened the card) to raise your rate.

In 2009, you better believe more and more credit card companies are going to jump to increase a low rate on a credit card if you make them nervous in any way. And just to be clear: An unpaid balance makes them nervous. Paying the minimum makes them nervous. Seeing you fall behind on another debt payment or missing a payment makes them nervous big-time.

If you want to steer clear of being hit with a giant rate hike, you have two options: don't run up a balance in the first place; or, if you do have an unpaid balance, get it paid off. When you have a zero balance, what do you care about the interest rate?

SITUATION: **You have a low-interest-rate credit card you never use—it is just there in case of emergency. Now you're worried that if you have to use it, your interest rate will go up.**

ACTION: Build a real emergency savings account. Relying on your credit card to bail you out of emergencies is too dangerous in 2009. (See "Action Plan: Saving" for advice on where to open a savings account and "Action Plan: Spending" for action steps on how to come up with more money to put toward a savings fund.)

If you use a credit card for an emergency expense in 2009 and you can't pay off the balance, you will set off a vicious cycle. An unpaid balance where there once was none makes a credit card company nervous. It can also make other credit card companies you have accounts with nervous. That could cause the credit limits on all your cards to be cut. And if that causes your FICO credit score to drop, then you can expect the interest rate on your credit card to rise.

The only solution is to stop thinking of your credit card as a safety net if you run into trouble. The only true safety net is a savings account.

SITUATION: You have a FICO credit score above 720 but your interest rate just shot up. What's the best way to pay off your credit card debt?

ACTION: See if you can apply for a balance transfer to a low-rate card. Because you have a high FICO score, you may be in luck. But lenders aren't exactly rolling out the welcome mat right now, so this may not be feasible.

Go to cardtrak.com and use the Search tool to shop for balance-transfer offers. The idea is to move your money to a card with a low introductory rate and then push yourself to get the balance paid off before the low rate expires. This can be tricky in 2009. You have the added risk that even if you do everything right with your new card, you could still have the introductory rate rescinded because something out of your control happened on one of your other accounts, such as having your credit limit reduced. In "Action Plan: Spending," I explain how to reassess your family's income and expenses to find more money to put toward paying down credit card debt.

SITUATION: You have a low FICO credit score, but you are current on all your accounts. How should you deal with your debt?

ACTION: Here's how:

- Pay the minimum amount due on every card each month. That's your only shot at keeping your FICO score from falling further. It will also lower the odds that your credit card company will close your account.
- Line up your cards and put the card that charges the highest interest rate at the top of the pile. That's the card you focus on paying off first. Send in as much money as you can each month to get that balance down to zero.
- Once the first card is paid off, focus on the second card in your pile: the card with the next-highest interest rate.
- Keep up with this system until you have all the cards paid off.

Of course, the big challenge is finding extra money every month to put toward paying off your credit card debt. In "Action Plan: Spending," I have suggestions about how to "find" more money in your month by reducing your expenses.

SITUATION: You are behind on your credit card payments, but you want to know the best payment strategy for improving your FICO score.

ACTION: Focus on paying the most you can on accounts that are the least late. The longer unpaid debt has been on your credit reports, the less effect it has on your FICO score. So if you can make current an account that is past due by only 60 days, it will help your FICO score far more than paying off your balance on an account you have been past due on for three years. I want you to organize your credit card statements into two piles: cards that are past due for less than one year and those that are past due for more than one year. Start with the first pile: Pay off the account that is closest to being current first, then move to the next card in that pile. Once you have paid off the cards in the first pile, I want you to use the strategy I covered in the action step above for paying off cards that you are more than one year behind on.

SITUATION: You want to use your HELOC to pay off your credit card debt.

ACTION: Do not do this. Even if you still have enough equity to keep your HELOC open, this is a dangerous mistake. You are putting your house at risk. When you borrow from your HELOC, your home is the collateral. Let's say you get laid off in 2009—not exactly impossible, given the way the economy is struggling—and suddenly you can't keep up with the HELOC payments on top of all your other bills. Fall behind on the payments and you could lose your house.

As much as I want you to pay off your credit card debt, you need to understand that credit card debt is "unsecured" debt. There is no collateral that a credit card company can easily force you to hand over to settle your debt. So it makes no sense to transfer your unsecured debt into a secured debt—a HELOC—where you run the risk of losing your home if you can't make the payments.

SITUATION: You want to take out a loan from your 401(k) to pay off your credit card debt.

ACTION: Do not do this. I know it is tempting, but it is such a dangerous move. Anyone who has been listening to my advice over the years knows I have never approved of 401(k) loans because you end up paying tax twice on the money you borrow. But I can understand that if you are staring at an interest rate of 30% on your credit card, you figure the tax penalty is worth paying.

Given what has happened to the economy, I once again must say no. First, we are in the midst of a severe recession. That increases the possibility that you will lose your job. I don't care how valued an employee you are. No one is safe when a company is losing money, or can't keep operating because the credit crisis makes it impossible for the firm to do business. We are all vulnerable in times like these. And if you have an outstanding loan against your 401(k) when you are laid off, you typically must pay off the loan within a short period of time. Fail to do that and it becomes a withdrawal; that means you owe tax on the entire amount immediately and a 10% early-withdrawal penalty if you are under age 55 in the year you left service. And tell me exactly where you will get the money for that. Not your credit card, that's for sure.

An even bigger issue is that you need your 401(k) for tomorrow. Use it today and what will you have in retirement? Can't think about that right now? Excuse me, you can't afford *not* to think about that. And that brings me to the issue of bankruptcy. I certainly hope this never happens to you, but in the event you must declare bankruptcy, one silver lining is that any money you have in a 401(k) or IRA is protected. That is, you will not be required to use your retirement savings to settle your debts. It is a permanent asset for you. Don't blow it by using the money to pay off your credit card debt.

SITUATION: You have heard that credit card companies may be willing to reach a settlement for a reduced payment. Who's a likely candidate?

ACTION: You must be seriously behind in your payments and have a sizable lump sum of cash at the ready to have any shot at working out a settlement that reduces what you owe.

The only way the credit card company will forgive a portion of your unpaid balance is if you can make a lump-sum payment that covers some of the money you owe. Let's say you have $20,000 in credit card debt that the credit card company is willing to reduce to $10,000. You need to be able to pay cold cash to cover the remaining $10,000 immediately. This is not about getting your balance lowered and then promising to be a good Boy Scout or Girl Scout who will stick to a monthly repayment plan. To get a settlement requires having enough cash at the ready to pay off the entire remaining (reduced) balance. If you don't have that money, you aren't likely to be offered a settlement deal.

SITUATION: You wonder if negotiating a settlement will hurt your FICO credit score.

ACTION: If you don't want your FICO score to go down, do not ask for a settlement. A settlement means you failed to live up to your obligation to pay the full amount of debt you were responsible for. It will indeed have a negative impact on your credit score. That said, in certain rare instances—if you've previously had a stellar record, have suffered a job loss or medical catastrophe, and the outstanding debt isn't huge—you may be able to convince the card issuer not to report the settlement. Be prepared to document your case.

SITUATION: You just received a tax document from the credit card company that says it reported the amount of your settlement to the IRS.

ACTION: Be prepared to pay income tax on the amount of the forgiven credit card debt.

By law, the credit card company is required to send you and the IRS a 1099-C form that shows the amount of the forgiven debt, which is indeed money that you will owe income tax on. Sorry, there is no tax break for credit card settlements. (An exception is if you are insolvent, meaning the amount of all your liabilities is more than the value of all your assets. If the forgiven debt is reported to the IRS on a Form 1099, you should attach a note to your tax return explaining the insolvency—otherwise, the IRS will likely initiate an automatic audit, since the income reported on the 1099 does not appear on your return. Be prepared with good documentation to back up your claim that at the time the debt was forgiven, your liabilities exceeded the fair market value of your assets. I recommend you work with a tax advisor to help you navigate this situation.)

SITUATION: You hold a credit card from a bank that failed. What's going to happen to your account?

ACTION: The best protection is a strong FICO score. When one bank fails, another bank takes on its existing credit card accounts. But you need to realize that the new bank is not required to keep offering you that card. It will investigate your account and decide if you are a good credit risk. And let's be honest here: If your bank failed in part because it was too lenient about extending credit, it stands to reason that the acquiring bank may not want to keep your business. Bottom line: If you are a credit risk, your credit card could be shut down. If you have a strong FICO score, you will no doubt be welcomed by the new bank with open arms.

SITUATION: You hold a credit card from a bank that failed. Do you still need to pay off your balance?

ACTION: Of course you are still responsible for the debt. People, there is no shortcut around personal responsibility. You made the charges, so you are responsible for the debt you ran up.

Keep sending in your payments. Print a copy of the canceled check or e-payment and keep it in a safe place. Chances are the transition to your new bank will be seamless, but you never know. I think it is wise to keep a printed record for at least six months after your bank has been taken over by another bank.

SITUATION: You have a FICO credit score of 660, but you were just turned down for a car loan.

ACTION: Improve your score to 720 if you want a loan with decent terms.

Lenders are no longer eager to lend money to people with just so-so credit. That's true of any type of loan: mortgages, car loans, private student loans. In the past (the days of irresponsible, subprime lending, circa 2007 and earlier), it was fairly easy for anyone to get a loan of any type. If you had a great FICO score over 720, you got the best terms. But if you had a low FICO score, you could still get a loan, though you'd pay a higher interest rate and maybe higher fees. Now a low score can mean no loan. It's the same issue we have been talking about over and over: Lenders are running for safety. They are very cautious about whom they will lend to. A FICO score below 700 is likely going to make it very hard to qualify for a loan in 2009, or you will have to pay a steep risk penalty: much higher interest rates and fees than you might have paid with the same score two years ago.

SITUATION: You want to improve your FICO credit score, but you aren't sure what to do.

ACTION: Know what matters to FICO and make the necessary changes in your financial life.

Fair Isaac is the parent company that is responsible for the FICO credit score. You actually have three FICO scores, one from each of the three credit bureaus: Equifax, Experian, and TransUnion. Credit scores range from 300 to 850. A year ago, I would have told you that a score of 720 or better was all you needed to get the best loan offers. But the fallout from the credit crisis has meant that the top tier has actually been pushed higher; some mortgage lenders reserve their best rates for individuals with FICO scores above 760. Unless you plan on buying a house in 2009, I wouldn't worry as long as your score is at least 720. That's still plenty good enough to keep most creditors happy.

If your score is below 720, here's what you need to do to make it better:

- **Pay bills on time.** This accounts for 35% of your credit score. If you are late on payments—not just credit card payments, but bills of any kind, it will pull down your score. Pay on time, even if it is just the minimum due, and it will help your score.
- **Reduce what you owe.** We already covered this earlier in the chapter. The less you owe on your cards and other debt, the less "risky" you look

to potential lenders. How much you owe relative to your available credit and other debts accounts for 30% of your score.

- **Hold on to cards with a long credit history.** The longer your credit record, the more data FICO has to assess whether you are a good credit risk. This accounts for 15% of your score. Make sure you keep your card with the longest history in good shape; you don't want it to be canceled.
- **Limit your credit applications.** The more new credit you ask for, the more nervous you make lenders. New credit accounts for 10% of your FICO score. If your record shows you have applied for multiple credit cards and a new car loan at the same time, it will pull down your score.
- **Aim for a mix of different types of credit.** I know this sounds crazy after explaining how you don't want to have too much credit, but lenders do in fact like to see that you have a few different types of credit. It's a sign you have experience juggling different obligations with different loan terms. So having a credit card and a car loan is actually better than having just a credit card. That said, your credit mix accounts for just 10% of your FICO score. And my advice for 2009 is to ignore this factor. If you have only credit cards, I am not going to suggest you sign up for a store card or take on some other debt.

SITUATION: You are considering hiring a debt-consolidation company to help you with your credit card debt.

ACTION: Don't fall for the come-ons. These offers are often rip-offs and can do serious damage to your credit score and leave you in more debt than you started with.

I know how tempting it sounds when you hear an ad that tells you the Super Duper Debt Consolidation Co. is standing by to make all your credit card debt stress go away. What they don't explain is that they typically charge you 10% or so of what you owe to take on your case, and in the event they work out a settlement with your creditors, they are going to want another 10% or more of the amount they "saved" you. And I promise you, these debt-consolidation companies aren't going to spend a lot of time explaining to you that any settlement they negotiate for you will ruin your FICO credit score and may end up costing you income tax on the amount of debt that is forgiven.

Most troubling is the growing number of complaints in 2008 that debt-consolidation firms collected their initial fee and then did nothing for the consumer. Not only were the clients out their fee, their FICO scores were hurt even more because the debt-consolidation firm told them they were taking care of the payments and the settlement. In reality, nothing was being done, so the amount owed ballooned as interest rates were raised and penalty fees piled up.

There is no easy way out of debt. Anyone promising to magically make everything all better is either lying to you or not explaining the financial and credit costs of what they are doing.

SITUATION: You don't know where to turn for honest help in dealing with your credit card debt.

ACTION: Contact the National Foundation for Credit Counseling. This is a network of nonprofit agencies with trained counselors who will help you assess your situation and lay out the most logical and realistic steps for you to follow. They are not miracle workers; as we just discussed, there are no miracles to be had when it comes to your credit card debt. But the NFCC are the "good guys" you can trust. Go to nfcc.org or call 800-388-2227.

SITUATION: You visited an NFCC-network credit counselor in 2008, but you still can't afford a repayment plan with credit card interest rates at 19%—and higher.

ACTION: Don't give up. In 2009, you may have more options. As I write, the NFCC has been working with the top ten card issuers on a plan to standardize a Debt Repayment Plan (DMP) by March 31, 2009 that would offer interest rates low enough so consumers could pay off their enrolled balances (with a fixed payment of 2% or a hardship payment of 1.75%) within five years. Check my Web site or nfcc.org for updates.

SITUATION: You feel the walls caving in and fear bankruptcy is your only option.

ACTION: Contact the NFCC and get honest help in assessing your options. If you aren't eligible for a DMP, the counselor will try to find a workable alternative to bankruptcy. Only about 10% of their clients have ended up in bankruptcy.

That said, if in fact you owe more than what you make; if you have tried every which way to pay your bills, including working a second or even a third job; if your debt keeps growing and you are being charged 32% interest and you can't see any way out, then bankruptcy may, sadly, be an option for you. Just remember that bankruptcy will destroy your FICO credit score, but then again, if you have been behind in payments your FICO score is probably already pretty low. Bankruptcy is really a last resort when you have tried everything else. This drastic step requires the most careful consideration. You will want to find a reputable attorney who can explain the current law, the pros and cons of filing, and the different kinds of bankruptcy. For a good overview of the subject visit the credit.com Web site at: www.credit.com/slp/chapter8/Bankruptcy.jsp.

SITUATION: You keep getting calls saying that you owe money on a credit card, but you have no idea what the collection agency is talking about.

ACTION: First of all, verify the debt. Debt collection agencies can pursue old debts that have never been paid off, hoping you will pay money to stop the calls. But plenty of times the debts are false—the result of identity theft, clerical errors, or credit reports that have not been updated. Sometimes a debt is so old it's passed the time period when a debt collector could legally sue to collect (see below). Within 30 days of being contacted, send the collector a letter (be sure to send it certified mail, return receipt requested) stating you do not owe the money, and requesting proof the debt is valid (such as a copy of the bill you supposedly owe). If the collection agency doesn't verify the debt within 30 days, it can no longer keep contacting you and cannot list the debt on your credit report. Remember your best shot at avoiding these "zombie" debts that erroneously resurface is by staying on top of your credit report. In these credit-crunched times, no one can afford a single inaccuracy that could lower a credit score. Go to annualcreditreport.com to get your free credit report. Each of the three credit bureaus, Equifax, Experian, and Transunion, are required to provide you with one free report a year.

SITUATION: You haven't been able to pay your credit card bills for some time and your cards were shut down five years ago, but you are still getting calls saying you owe money.

ACTION: Check out your state's statute of limitations on debt collection. In every state, the statue of limitations for credit card debt begins to tick from the date you failed to make a payment that was due—as long as you never made another payment on that credit card account. (You can find the list of state statutes at http://www.fair-debt-collection.com/SOL-by-State.html#15.) One way to prove the statute applies to your debts is to get a copy of your credit report. It will list the dates you were delinquent as reported by your creditors. So if your state's statute of limitations on credit card debt is five years, and your last payment was due on April 12, the statute of limitations on that debt will run out five years from that April 12, assuming you haven't made another payment. (Please note: statutes will vary for different types of debt. The statutes of limitations are different for credit card accounts than for mortgages and auto loans.) Also important to note: If you are contacted by a collection agency and you make a promise to send in a check or you actually do send in a small amount of money, it is possible that the statute of limitations starts all over again.

SITUATION: You are being harrassed at work by calls from collection agencies.

ACTION: The Fair Debt Collection Practices Act (FDCPA) restricts tactics that debt collection agencies may use. They cannot call you at work if they know your employer prohibits such calls. Once you tell them this, they have to stop the calls; it's wise to follow up with a letter. Show you know your rights by informing them that under provision 15 of the U.S. Code, section 1692b-c, the letter constitutes formal notice to stop all future communications with you except for the reasons specifically set forth in the federal law. Collectors also cannot phone your home so often as to constitute harassment and they cannot call before 8 A.M. or after 9 P.M. You can learn more about your rights under the FDCPA at http://www.credit.com/credit_information/credit_law/Understanding-Your-Debt-Collection-Rights.jsp#2.

4

ACTION PLAN

Retirement Investing

The New Reality

After watching your 401(k) and IRA investments lose 30% or more last year, you are consumed with fear and doubt. You fear that your losses are so steep you will never be able to afford a comfortable retirement. And you doubt that you will ever be able to recover those losses, especially if you stick with stocks. I completely understand why you would feel that way.

But I have to tell you, the biggest risk to your retirement security is giving in to your emotions. When fear and doubt are in control, you may make decisions that feel "right" for 2009, but they will hurt your long-term retirement strategy. That's what makes retirement investing so tough: You need to have the resolve and confidence to look past what is happening this month, this quarter, and this year, and focus instead on the correct actions to take today that will serve you well in retirement.

For many of you, the toughest thing I will ask of you in 2009 is not to change a thing. As I will explain, sticking to your long-term strategy in 2009 is more important—and has the potential to have the greatest payoff down the line—than in any other year.

At the same time, those of you who are within 10 years or so of retiring may need to make big changes to your retirement strategy. I've heard from so many near-retirees, panicking now because they had the bulk of their money invested in stocks. As I will explain in detail in the Action Plan that follows, that was never a good idea. As you near retirement, you need to begin shifting greater and greater portions of your money into bonds and stable-value accounts.

I cannot stress enough how important it is to be careful about retirement investing in 2009. Rash actions are not the right actions. Trust me, you cannot afford to get this wrong. So please read what follows carefully. Whether you are 25 or 65, I have laid out the actions you need to take to stay on course, starting now.

What You Must Do in 2009

- Make sure you have the right mix of stocks and bonds in your retirement accounts given your age.
- Do not make early withdrawals or take loans from retirement accounts to pay for non-retirement expenses.
- Convert an old 401(k) to a rollover IRA so you can invest in the best low-cost funds, ETFs, and bonds.
- If eligible in 2009, consider moving at least a portion of a 401(k) rollover into a Roth IRA. Or wait until 2010 to convert to a Roth, when everyone, regardless of income, will be able to make this move. Just be aware of the tax due at conversion.

Your 2009 Action Plan: Retirement Investing

PLEASE NOTE: *When I refer to 401(k)s throughout this chapter, the advice is also applicable to 403(b)s and other tax-deferred accounts.*

SITUATION: You don't plan on retiring for at least 10 years, but after watching your retirement account lose 30% in 2008 you've had it with stocks. You want to stop investing in the stock market, at least until you see stocks going up again.

ACTION: Resist the temptation to stop investing in stocks. If you have time on your side—and that means at least 10 years, and preferably longer, before you need money—you want to keep a large portion of your retirement money in stocks.

As noted above, the hardest part of retirement investing is staying focused on your long-term goal, rather than getting overwhelmed by what is happening day-to-day. And if your goal is indeed 10, 20, or 30 years off in the future, then I have to tell you that now looks like a great time to keep investing in stocks. I know that's hard to fathom when stock prices are so low, but it's because they are much lower that the long-term prospects are for better performance. You remember the first commandment of investing—buy low, sell high? Well, right now you can definitely buy at lower prices. I am not suggesting that you will be able to sell higher next year or even the year after. That's not likely. But it is also irrelevant, because we are focusing on the opportunity to buy today and hold for 10, 15, 20 years or more. Buy low today and down the road it's likely you will be able to sell at much higher levels.

SITUATION: You keep hearing that the best thing you can do is to keep investing in your 401(k), but it just makes no sense to you, given that 2009 is supposed to be a rocky year in the markets.

ACTION: Focus on how many shares you can buy in 2009 and forget about the value of those shares.

If you have time on your side, and by that I mean at least 10 years until you intend to tap your retirement savings, your concern should not be so much what your retirement accounts are worth today but what they might be worth in the future.

I understand the desire to shift all your money into a stable-value fund or money market fund offered in your 401(k). But that is a short-term salve that could leave you weaker in the long run. Why? Because once you move your money out of stocks, you give up any chance to make back your losses. Sure, the stable-value fund will inch along with a 3% to 4% gain each year, but chances are that's not enough to help you reach your long-term investing goals; the return of a stable-value fund will barely keep up with the rate of inflation. If you told me your account was already large enough that simply keeping pace with inflation was all you needed, then I would be the first to say: Move everything into the stable-value fund. But that's not the situation most people are in; they need larger gains over time to build a big enough retirement pot to retire comfortably. Only stocks offer the potential for inflation-beating gains over the long term.

As I write in mid-November 2008, many of the major stock indexes are down 40% over the past year. While there could definitely be additional losses as we work our way out of the credit mess and economic recession, I believe we have probably seen the worst of the damage. I do not expect us to be down another 40% from here.

SITUATION: You have more than 10 years before retirement, but you just can't stand to watch your 401(k) go down every month. You want to put your monthly contributions in a safe place within your retirement account.

ACTION: You have to understand that at today's lower prices, the money you continue to invest in your 401(k) will buy more shares. And what you want right now is to gather as many shares as you can. Now, I am not a wishful thinker; I certainly expect more instability in the markets in 2009 that could push stock prices even lower. So why would I tell you to keep buying in 2009? Because it is going to pay off for you in 2019 and 2029 and 2039.

Let's walk through a simplified hypothetical example. Let's say you invested $200 in your 401(k)'s stock fund. The share price was $20, so your $200 bought 10 shares. One month later, let's say that the share price has fallen to $10 a share. That means your $200 can buy you 20 shares.

If, however, you decided to give up on the stock market after that one month of investing and put your $200 contribution into a stable-value fund, you would still own your 10 shares and have $200 in cash in your 401(k).

On the other hand, if you decided to keep investing your $200 contribution that month into the stock fund at $10 a share, you would now have 30 shares—the 10 you bought the first month and the 20 you bought the second.

Now, for the purposes of this exercise, let's assume that the stock fund went back up to $20 a share one month after you did this.

In the first example, where you stopped investing in the stock market, your 10 shares at $20 would now be worth $200 and you would still have $200 in the stable-value fund. So in total you would have $400 in your account. You broke even.

In the second scenario, if you kept investing, you would now have 30 shares of the stock fund in your 401(k) that is now worth $20 a share. You would now have $600 in your account—a gain of $200 over what you invested.

In the first example, you are just back to where you started. In the second, you are up 50% on your money.

I realize this is an extreme example—there is no chance your stock investments will completely rebound in one month—but I wanted to make the point clearly that the right action to take over time is invest, invest, invest. As long as you have at least 10 years until you need this money, I am telling you to try to relax and have a long-term perspective when you open your statement and the value of your account has gone down. The more it goes down, the more shares you get to buy; the more shares you buy now, the bigger the payoff when the market goes back up. Please do not stop investing now. Don't change your strategy—just change your point of view.

SITUATION: Your plan is to get out of stocks while they continue to go down, then shift your money back to stocks when things get better.

ACTION: What you are trying to do is "market timing." In the short term, you may feel as if you are doing the right thing, but it will backfire on you over the long term. And retirement investing is all about the long term.

The big problem with market timing is that if you are out of the stock market, you run the very real risk that you will not be back in the market when it rallies; there is no way you will ever make up for your losses if you miss those rallies.

Listen, I get where you're coming from: It would be so great if we could sell before the markets go down and buy before the markets go back up, but it is nearly impossible to have perfect timing because there is no telling when the big rallies will come. For example, one day in an extremely wild period in October 2008, the Dow Jones Industrial Average lost nearly 700 points. Let's say you got out of stocks that day because you had had enough.

Well, two trading days later the Dow Jones Industrial Average skyrocketed more than 900 points. So you missed the rally that wiped out the losses from a few days earlier. Of course, that is a very rare and dramatic example; it's not often we get such huge swings in the space of a few trading days. But the point is clear: If you try to time the markets, you risk missing out on rallies.

I know it is not fun or easy, but a long-term buy-and-hold strategy in a diversified mutual fund or exchange-traded fund (ETF) is what works best. Here's some evidence to consider:

Let's say you invested $1,000 in 1950 and then had perfect market timing and managed to miss the 20 worst months between 1950 and June 2008. Your $1,000 would have grown to more than $800,000, according to Toreador Research & Trading. But it's not as if there is some public calendar that tells us exactly when to get in and out. So let's take a look at what happens if you missed the 20 best months for stocks during that stretch—that is, you were in cash when the market rallied. Well, your $1,000 would have grown to just $11,500. If, instead, you had invested your $1,000 and left it in the market through good and bad times, you would have ended up with more than $73,000. Sure, that's a lot less than $800,000. But it's also a lot more than $11,500. Granted, none of us think in terms of a 57-year time horizon, but please know that myriad studies similar to this one come to the same conclusion over shorter time spans too. Buy and hold is the sweet spot between elusive perfect market timing and tragic poor market timing.

SITUATION: You have time on your side, but you still don't trust history this time. You just can't shake the feeling that this time is different, that buy-and-hold investing is not the way to go.

ACTION: Push yourself to keep the faith. But if at the end of the day you can't function because you are so worried, then perhaps it is best for you to get out of stocks. However, you need to understand the serious trade-off you will make.

Let's start by stripping away your emotions for a moment. My best financial advice is for you to stay invested. I know what we are going through right now is incredibly scary. But we have had scary times before.

On the next page are the 10 most recent bear markets (periods of major losses when the stock market indexes go down at least 20%) prior to 2008.

So this is not the first (or last) scary time. What's crucial to understand is that despite all those bad times, patient investors did fine. More than fine, actually. From 1950 through 2007, the annualized gain for the S&P 500 stock index was more than 10%. The big takeaway: There are bad times and there are good times, and history tells us that over time, the good times outweigh the bad.

BEAR MARKET	LOSS
August 1956–October 1957	−21.6%
December 1961–June 1962	−28%
February 1966–October 1966	−22%
November 1968–May 1970	−36%
January 1973–October 1974	−48.2%
September 1976–March 1978	−19.4%
January 1981–August 1982	−25.85
August 1987–December 1987	−33.5%
July 1990–October 1990	−19.9%
March 2000–October 2002	−49.1%

Source: The Vanguard Group; Standard & Poor's

So now you know my best financial advice: Stay the course. That is what I would do if it were my money. But it's not my money. It's *your* money. And no one will ever care about your money as much as you do. So if you know that the only way you can get through these tough times is to pull your money out of stocks and into a stable-value fund or a money market, then you need to do that. I just ask that you consider everything you read in this Action Plan. From a financial point of view, you are putting yourself at the risk of never making up the losses and not making big enough gains to beat inflation. Perhaps you can strike a compromise with yourself: How about you move a small percentage of your money out of stocks and into a stable-value fund? That will make it easier to get through the rocky times, but it will keep a portion of your retirement funds invested in stocks.

I respect the emotional component of investing—something that too many professionals dismiss. All I ask of you in 2009 is to try as hard as you can not to let your emotions completely derail your long-term strategy. Compromise could be the ticket for you: By moving a portion of your money into a stable-value fund—say, no more than a third or so—you should be able to sleep better today without derailing your chances of sleeping well in retirement too.

SITUATION: You want to stop contributing to your 401(k), even though your company matches your contribution, so you will have more money to pay off your credit card debt.

ACTION: Don't do it. If you work for a company that matches your contribution, I don't care how much credit card debt you have or how messy your financial life may be. You cannot afford to miss out on a company match. Do you hear me?

When your employer matches a dollar of your money with a 25-cent matching contribution or gves you 50 cents for a dollar invested that is too good a deal to pass up.

SITUATION: You want to stop contributing to your 401(k) after you reach the maximum employer match so you will have more money to pay off your credit card debt.

ACTION: Do it. Once you get to the point where you have maxed out your employer's matching contribution (ask HR to help you figure out the max you need to contribute to collect the full company match), then you absolutely should stop contributing so you have more money in your paycheck to put toward paying off your credit cards. As I explain in "Action Plan: Credit," reducing your credit card balances is not only smart in 2009, it is necessary.

SITUATION: You plan on retiring in five years and are wondering if it makes more sense to keep contributing to your 401(k) or use the money to pay off your mortgage.

ACTION: If you intend to live in your home forever, then I recommend you focus on paying off the mortgage. With one big caveat: If you get a company match on your 401(k), you must keep investing enough to qualify for the maximum employer match. That is a great deal you are not to pass up. But I wholeheartedly recommend scaling back your contribution rate just to the point of the match so that you'll have more money in your paycheck to put toward paying off your mortgage before you retire. Yes, I realize this means you will have less saved in your 401(k), but you will also need a lot less because you will no longer have a mortgage payment to deal with in retirement, and for most retirees that is the biggest income worry.

SITUATION: **You can't afford your mortgage and want to borrow or withdraw money from your 401(k) to make the payments.**

ACTION: Don't do it. Too many people these days are making this huge mistake. I understand that you are desperate to hang on to your house and will do anything to avoid foreclosure, but I definitely do not want you to take a withdrawal. You will pay income tax and may also be hit with a 10% penalty for money taken out before you are 59½. And then, six months later, you will find yourself back in the same hole: All the money from your 401(k) will be gone and once again you will fall behind on your mortgage.

A 401(k) loan carries a ton of risk, too. If you are laid off, you typically must pay back the loan within a few months. The current economic outlook predicts a rise in layoffs in 2009. So if you take out the loan, get laid off, and can't pay the money back ASAP, you will run into another tax problem: The loan is treated as a withdrawal and you'll be stuck paying tax—and possibly a 10% early-withdrawal penalty. A loan is also dangerous because the markets may rally during the time you have taken out the loan, which means you will have missed an important period to recoup some of your losses.

It's also important to know that money you have in a 401(k) or IRA is protected if you ever have to file for bankruptcy. You get to keep that money no matter what.

My preference is that you scour every part of your financial life to find other income sources for covering your mortgage. See "Action Plan: Spending" for advice on how to squeeze more savings out of your current income.

SITUATION: Your credit card account was closed down and your interest rate on the remaining balance was increased to 32%. You want to take a 401(k) loan to wipe out the credit card debt.

ACTION: As noted above, it is just too risky to take out a loan from your 401(k) in 2009, given the heightened possibility of layoffs. I understand the damage a 32% credit card interest rate can do, but I want you to resist the temptation to raid your 401(k). Please review "Action Plan: Spending" for my advice on how to seriously tackle your expenses to find savings you can then put toward important financial goals, such as paying off high-rate credit card debt.

SITUATION: You have been laid off and need the money in your 401(k). Can you withdraw it without paying the 10% penalty?

ACTION: Yes, if you are 55 years of age or older in the year you were laid off. You will, however, still have to pay ordinary income tax on what you withdraw. I want to be clear: I am not recommending that you take money out of your retirement accounts at such a young age, but I recognize that some of you are in a very tough situation. I'm asking that you please do everything you can to avoid tapping your retirement money today.

SITUATION: You are under 55 in the year you were laid off. You desperately need the money in your retirement account just to make ends meet. Is there a way you can withdraw it without having to pay the 10% penalty?

ACTION: Yes. But it is tricky. Look into setting up a withdrawal plan that allows you to take out substantial and equal periodic payments (SEPP) from your retirement account without paying the 10% penalty. Please check with your tax advisor so he or she can tell you exactly how it works—it is covered by Rule 72t in the IRS code—and make sure your advisor is an expert in this area, because it is very complicated. This applies to all kinds of retirement accounts, not just 401(k)s and 403(b)s as the situation above does. And I need to repeat what I said above: Taking money out of your retirement account at an early age is obviously not ideal. So please do everything possible to leave your retirement money untouched.

SITUATION: You are worried that your company may go bankrupt and that you will lose all the money in your 401(k).

ACTION: Confirm that your money was sent from your employer to your 401(k) plan and you have nothing to worry about. Money you invest in a 401(k) is your money, not your employer's. Your employer hires a third party—typically a brokerage, fund company, or insurance company—to run the 401(k), and that company in turn segregates your money in a separate account that is all yours; even if that brokerage or fund company got into trouble.

SITUATION: You have employer matching contributions that are not fully vested and you are concerned that you may lose this money if your company goes bankrupt.

ACTION: That could indeed happen. Money that is not vested is not yet yours. So in the event your company goes under, it is not legally obligated to leave the unvested portion of your match in your account. The money *you* contribute to your 401(k) is always 100% yours.

SITUATION: Your employer announced it will suspend its 401(k) matching contributions in 2009. Should you keep contributing to your 401(k)?

ACTION: Because you are not going to get the matching contribution, you want to be strategic about how best to use your money. If you have credit card debt, suspend your 401(k) contributions so you have more money in your paycheck to put toward paying off your credit card balance. If you do not have credit card debt but you do not have an eight-month emergency fund, make sure you create a savings fund before you do anything else. If you have no credit card debt and you have an eight-month emergency fund, then I suggest you suspend your 401(k) contributions in 2009 and instead—if you qualify—invest in a Roth IRA account. If you don't qualify, invest in a traditional IRA. If you already have funded your Roth or IRA, then just keep taking that extra money to pay down the mortgage on your home if you plan to stay in that home forever or keep contributing to your 401(k); even without the company match, it remains a smart way to save tax-deferred for your retirement.

SITUATION: You have money in an old employer's 401(k) and wonder if you should leave it where it is, transfer it to your new employer's plan, or do an IRA rollover.

ACTION: Do an IRA rollover. Rather than be restricted to the handful of mutual funds offered in your 401(k), you get to pick the funds, exchange-traded funds (ETFs), and stocks or individual bonds to invest in when you do an IRA rollover. That puts you in total control and allows you to choose the best low-cost investments for your retirement money.

SITUATION: You want to do an IRA rollover, but you don't know how.

ACTION: Choose the financial institution you want to move your money to (that's the rollover part) and that company will help you switch the money from the 401(k) into your new IRA account. I believe keeping your costs as low as possible is vitally important, so I recommend discount brokerages or no-load fund companies that also have a low-cost brokerage arm for your bond and ETF investing. Once you pick the firm you want to move your money to, all you will need to do is complete an easy rollover application form and choose the option for a direct rollover; that means your new firm will contact your old 401(k) directly and get your money moved. Once your IRA is in place, set up an automated monthly investment (from a bank account) for the growth portion of your retirement portfolio. I highly recommend making monthly investments rather than big, once-a-year lump-sum investments. Periodic investments are a way to dollar cost average, a smart investment strategy for stock investing.

SITUATION: You want to do an IRA rollover but are not sure if you should roll it over into a traditional IRA or a Roth IRA.

ACTION: If you are eligible to roll over into a Roth IRA in 2009, you have to consider it. There is one big caveat, though: When you convert any money into a Roth IRA that was in either a 401(k) or a traditional IRA, you will owe taxes. So you need to consider carefully how you will come up with the cash to cover a tax bill. One strategy is to convert just a small portion at a time, so you aren't hit with a staggering tax bill. I also highly recommend you consult a tax advisor with expertise in Roth conversions to make sure you choose a strategy that does not put you in a tax bind.

But here is what you need to understand: The money in your 401(k) is, in most instances, tax-deferred. That means when you eventually withdraw money from it in retirement, it will be taxed at your ordinary income tax rate. If you roll it over into a traditional IRA, the system stays the same for tax purposes.

A Roth IRA is different: You invest money that you have already paid tax on and then in retirement you get to take out all the money in your Roth without paying any tax on it. So the smart thing to do with your 401(k) is to roll it over first into an IRA rollover. Then, depending on how much money you actually have in your IRA rollover, you would either convert it to a Roth IRA little by little or do it all at once. Remember, you will owe taxes on whatever amount of money you convert. But if you go through this effort there is a nice payoff: The growth on the money in your Roth IRA will be tax-free if you leave it untouched until you are 59½ and have owned the Roth for at least five years. You can learn more about Roth conversions at http://www.fairmark.com/rothira.

SITUATION: **You want to convert to a Roth IRA but were told your income is too high.**

ACTION: Roll your 401(k) into a traditional IRA in 2009 and then convert that IRA into a Roth IRA in 2010, when everyone, regardless of income, will be allowed to convert to a Roth.

In 2009, you must have modified adjusted gross income (MAGI) below $100,000 on your federal tax return to be eligible for a Roth conversion. That's $100,000 whether you are single or you file a joint tax return. But the income limit vanishes in 2010; everyone and anyone will be allowed to convert their rollover 401(k) or traditional IRA into a Roth IRA in 2010. A nice bonus of waiting until 2010 is that any tax due on your conversion can be paid over two years.

SITUATION: You converted to a Roth IRA in 2008, but you are kicking yourself now because your account is down 20% and you owe tax on the amount that was originally converted.

ACTION: Do a recharacterization. In a rare act of leniency, the IRS allows for do-overs of IRA conversions. If you convert a traditional IRA to a Roth and then regret it, you get to reverse your decision.

The advantage of doing this during a down market is that you can then reconvert back into the Roth IRA and your new tax bill will be based on the current value of the account at the time of the second conversion.

So let's say you converted $20,000 in 2008. Then the market decline dropped the value to $10,000. You owe tax on the $20,000, since that was the value at the time of the conversion. If you do a recharacterization, the money goes back into the traditional IRA and you wipe out that tax bill. You must then wait until the next tax year to reconvert to a Roth. Let's assume at that point your IRA is still stuck at $10,000. You will owe tax on that $10,000 conversion. That's a lot better than the 2008 tax bill that would be based on the $20,000 original conversion.

SITUATION: You aren't sure if you qualify for a Roth, and how much you can contribute if you do.

ACTION: In 2009, the Roth contribution limit is $5,000 if you are under 50 years old; if you are above 50, you can invest up to $6,000. Individuals with modified adjusted gross income below $105,000 and married couples filing a joint tax return with income below $166,000 can invest up to those maximums. Individuals with income between $105,000 and $120,000 and married couples with income between $166,000 and $176,000 can make reduced contributions. Any financial institution that offers Roth IRAs will have an online calculator or a customer-service representative to help you determine your eligibility.

SITUATION: You qualify for a Roth, but you wonder why you should bother with one if you can just keep contributing to your 401(k) after you exceed the company match.

ACTION: It's important to understand that all the money you pull out of your 401(k) (or traditional IRA, for that matter) will be taxed at your ordinary income-tax rate. And given the large deficits our country faces—to say nothing of the large bills for various bailouts—there is every reason to believe that tax rates are going to be higher in the future, not lower. How do you protect yourself from those higher tax rates? Invest your retirement money in a Roth IRA. If the account has been open for at least five years and you are 59½ when you take it out, it will not be taxed, period. It is far better to pay taxes on your money today so you never have to pay them again. Also, it's helpful to know, especially in times like these, that you can always withdraw any money you originally contributed to your Roth at any time, without taxes or penalties, regardless of your age. Only the growth on your contributions must stay in your Roth until you are 59½. At that point, and if the account has been open for at least five years, you'll be able to withdraw the growth tax-free as well.

Another great benefit of a Roth is that if you do not need to make withdrawals, the IRS will not force you to; you can just leave the money growing and eventually pass it along to your heirs as an amazing tax-free inheritance. That's quite different from a traditional IRA and 401(k): The IRS insists you start making required minimum distributions no later than the year you turn 70½.

SITUATION: **Your income is too high to invest in a Roth IRA.**

ACTION: Invest in a traditional (nondeductible) IRA; even if you can't deduct your contribution, the money you set aside will grow tax-deferred in 2009 and then you can convert to a Roth IRA in 2010.

SITUATION: **You don't know how to invest the money you have in your retirement account.**

ACTION: You need a mix of stocks and bonds; the mix is mostly a function of how many years you have until you retire, but I also respect that your "risk tolerance" might affect your decision making. In the questions that follow, I tell you what percentage of stocks and bonds you should have if you are five years from retirement, 10 to 15 years from retirement, or 20 or more years from retirement.

EXCHANGE-TRADED FUNDS (ETFS) AND NO-LOAD MUTUAL FUNDS: *For your* *stock holdings, I'd like you to focus on either no-load index mutual funds, ETFs, or high-yielding, dividend-paying stocks. ETFs and no-load mutual funds are the best way to build a diversified portfolio. Each mutual fund or ETF owns dozens and often hundreds of stocks; for those of you who do not have large sums of money ($100,000 or more) to invest, that is a safer way to go than if you put all your money into a few individual stocks.*

BONDS: *I prefer you to invest in individual bonds, rather than bond funds. I'll explain below.*

SITUATION: You don't know which is better—a no-load mutual fund or an ETF?

ACTION: If your retirement account offers them, ETFs are the way to go.

Here's what you need to understand: Mutual funds and ETFs both charge what is known as an annual expense ratio. This is an annual fee that everyone pays, but it is sort of hidden in that you won't see it deducted from your account as a line-item cost; instead, it is shaved off of your fund's return. There are no-load index mutual funds that have very low expense ratios—below 0.30%. But ETFs can be even better, with annual expense ratios of as little as 0.07%. I know that sounds like a very small difference, but hey, every penny you keep in your account rather than pay as a fee is money that continues to grow for your retirement. That's just one reason why I love ETFs. The one catch with ETFs is that they trade on the stock markets as if they were a stock, so that means you will have to pay a commission to buy and sell ETF shares; when you buy a no-load mutual fund you do not pay a commission. Discount brokerages often charge $10 or so. That's not a big deal to pay a few times a year, but you sure don't want to pay that commission if you are making investments every month with small amounts of money (dollar cost averaging). If that's the case, you are better off putting money in your IRA every month into a money market account and then purchasing your ETFs every three months rather than every month. That way you save on commissions.

SITUATION: You want to invest in stocks, but you're confused by all the choices. What's a good long-term strategy?

ACTION: A solid long-term strategy for the stock portion of your portfolio is to put 90% of your stock money in a broad U.S. index fund or ETF and 10% in an international stock fund or ETF. The Vanguard Total Stock Market Index fund (VTSMX) and its ETF cousin, the Vanguard Total Stock Market ETF (VTI), are good choices for your U.S. investment. Now, if you are antsy about stocks in 2009, I want you to be sure to check out my advice later in this chapter for investing in high-dividend funds or ETFs. I think they are a great defensive way to invest in stocks in 2009, and it is perfectly fine to use dividend funds/ETFs instead of the U.S. index fund. For the international portion, you can opt for the Vanguard Total International Stock Index (VGTSX) or the iShares MSCI EAFE ETF (EFA).

PLEASE NOTE: *If you are currently invested in cash or bonds, and are ready to follow my strategy for owning stocks, don't rush to move all your money into stocks in one lump sum. I recommend you use the dollar-cost-averaging strategy explained in this chapter and invest equal amounts each month over the next year to move your money slowly into stocks.*

SITUATION: You aren't sure if the fixed-income portion of your money belongs in bonds or bond funds.

ACTION: Buy individual bonds if you can, not bond funds.

I prefer bonds to bond funds because with a high-quality bond you know you will get the amount you invested back once the bond matures. For example, if you invest $5,000 in a Treasury note with a five-year maturity, you will get the $5,000 back after the note matures in five years. During the time you own the note, you will also collect a fixed interest for all of those five years. (By the way, a note works just like a bond; it's just that our Treasury likes to call them notes.) The problem with bond funds is that they do not have a maturity date and their interest rate is not fixed. So you may get back less than what you invested and your interest rate could go down over the years.

I recommend keeping the bond portion of your account in Treasuries and/or CDs if you are in a retirement account, and high-quality general-obligation municipal bonds outside of a retirement account. Because of what is going on in the economy, I think it's wise to stick with notes or bonds that mature in five years or less. In the coming years, we may see higher interest rates, so I don't want you to lock up your money today for 10 years or longer. Stick with shorter maturities so you can reinvest at what I expect will be higher rates in the future. (If your money is in a 401(k) and you are five years or less from retirement, I have to say that in 2009 I think it is best to stick with the stable-value fund or the money market option, rather than the bond fund.)

SITUATION: You are five years away from retirement and you feel you cannot afford to lose one penny more in your 401(k) plan. What should you do?

ACTION: Ideally, you don't want to bail out of stocks completely. Let's review a few important issues. First, any money you know you will need in the next five to 10 years to pay bills does not belong in the stock market. Never has and never will. But just because you are retiring in five years, it doesn't mean you will need to use all that money immediately, right? Some you will start to use, and the rest you won't touch for 10 or 20 or even 30 years, given our longer life spans. If that sounds like your situation, I would ask you to think about keeping 25% to 30% of your money in stocks even if you are just five years from retirement.

If your issue is that you lost so much money you worry you won't have enough for retirement and you want to keep what you have safe, then you need to face facts. Moving all your money into a stable-value fund is not the solution. Here's what you need to do: Delay your retirement for another three years or more. That will give your stocks more time to recover from the recent losses. It will also potentially give you more working years to save more. And most important, it means you delay when you start to need the money; every year you can put off touching your retirement savings is going to be a tremendous help to you.

Now, the one exception here is if in fact you have determined that when you retire you want to use all your Roth IRA money to pay off your mortgage. In that case, you will indeed "need" all your money sooner rather than later. And to repeat myself: Money you know you need within five to 10 years does not belong in stocks. Put it all in your retirement plan's stable-value fund or money market account.

SITUATION: You are 10 years from retirement and you don't know how much should be invested in stocks and how much should be in bonds or cash.

ACTION: Keep at least 50% of your money in individual bonds, CDs, or stable-value funds or money market accounts. The absolute best move when you are nearing retirement is to reduce your risk, and that means moving out of stocks and into bonds. But this only makes sense if your stash at the point you retire is big enough that you can get by on it earning 4% or so a year from bond interest. You need to make sure you have a large enough amount saved up and you have figured your costs correctly to be able to move completely into bonds and live comfortably. It's also important to realize that even if you retire at 60, there's a very good chance you will live to be 80 or even 90. So you are asking your retirement fund to support you for 20 or 30 years. The simple math is that if you are making withdrawals from your retirement account each month and your remaining balance is growing at just 4% or so a year, you run the risk that your money will not last 25 or 30 years. (Just about every financial institution has a free online retirement calculator that will estimate how long your money will last. Or type "retirement calculator" into your search engine.) You need to balance the growth potential of stocks with the fact that you will soon be relying on your retirement account to live. A 50-50 mix is a good target for balancing those two different needs.

As I explain later in this chapter, I think ETFs that focus on dividend-paying stocks are a very smart place for your stock investments today. The income you receive from the dividend is a good way to "get paid" today while still investing in stocks for future gains. If you currently have a 50% stock investment and want to invest in dividend-paying stocks, you can make the switch over. If, however, you have a lot of money in bonds or cash, please take your time moving money into a stock ETF; rather than one lump-sum investment, make smaller monthly investments—known as dollar cost averaging—over the course of the next year.

SITUATION: You don't plan to touch your retirement money for 10 to 15 years. How much should be invested in stocks and how much should be in bonds/cash?

ACTION: If you have 15 years until retirement, have about 70% in stocks and then scale that back by 5 percentage points or so each year, so that when you are 10 years from retirement you have 50% in stocks.

SITUATION: You have 20 or more years until retirement and you want to know how much should be invested in stocks and how much should be in bonds/cash.

ACTION: Aim for 100% stocks. You are in a great situation. You have so much time on your hands that you can ride out this bear market and profit when the market rallies. As I said earlier, now may prove to be a fantastic time to be investing in stocks because you get to buy in at lower prices.

If you are afraid to have all your money in the market, there is nothing wrong with keeping 20% or so in bonds/cash. With that mix, you are going to do well when the stock markets rally and also have a nice bond cushion to reduce your portfolio's losses when the stock market is falling. If that helps you relax a bit and stay committed to a long-term strategy, I think 20% in bonds is just fine, but I'd prefer to be in stocks 100%.

SITUATION: You were planning on retiring in 2009, but after taking these big losses in your account you're not sure you can still afford to.

ACTION: Focus on what the market loss will mean to you in terms of monthly income.

Let's say in 2007 you had a $250,000 retirement stash. Today it is $200,000. So what does that mean to you in terms of retirement income? Your intention at retirement was to have your money invested mostly in bonds so your money would be safe and you could count on a return of approximately 4% in 2009. The $50,000 you lost would generate $2,000 in income at a 4% rate. In other words, your real monthly loss in income comes to about $170 a month. So the question is, does that loss of $170 a month mean you can no longer retire? If the answer to that question is yes, then the truth is you really were cutting it too close to retire anyway.

SITUATION: **You have an IRA at a brokerage firm, but you're worried that if the company goes under, as Bear Stearns did, you will lose all your money.**

ACTION: Stop worrying. The money you have invested in your accounts at a brokerage or fund company is completely separate from the operations of the parent company. The brokerage or fund company can't use your money to pay its bills and debt.

Even if a company goes under, what happens is that you will transfer your money to another brokerage or fund company. Or, more likely, the company will be taken over and you become a client of that new company.

And just so you know, if there is an irregularity and a company uses your money fraudulently, you may be able to recover up to $500,000 ($100,000 limit for cash accounts) from the Securities Investor Protection Corp. This is not like federal insurance. It's a voluntary program of member firms that keeps a kitty around to settle problems; at the end of 2007, SIPC had about $1.5 billion in its fund. This covers standard investment accounts only; SIPC does not cover alternatives such as currency and commodity investments. Check with your brokerage or fund company to see if it belongs to SIPC.

SITUATION: You have a variable annuity and are worried that the insurance company will go under and you will lose all your money.

ACTION: Money invested in a variable annuity is typically in segregated subaccounts that are separate from your insurer's balance sheet. Even if the insurer runs into trouble, your money should not be affected. Now, that said, you do need to understand that your variable annuity is susceptible to market losses; that's what the word "variable" means. How much your account is worth is largely a function of the performance of the subaccounts (funds) you are invested in.

SITUATION: You have a single-premium fixed annuity and are worried that the insurance company will go under and you will lose your money.

ACTION: With a single-premium fixed annuity your payout is indeed a guarantee from your insurer, so if your insurer goes under there is reason to be concerned. Concerned, but not panicked.

First, in the unlikely event anything happens to your insurer, there is a state guaranty fund that will swoop in to cover annuity payments—up to certain limits. In most states, the guaranteed payout for an annuity is $100,000, though it can be higher in some states. (Go to www.nohlga.com and use the locator to find your state's insurance department, where you can learn about your state's guaranty fund limits.)

If your annuity exceeds your state's guaranty limit, you need to weigh the cost of cashing out carefully.

SITUATION: You are retired and need a higher income payout than you can get from bank CDs today.

ACTION: Consider municipal bonds and dividend-paying stock mutual funds or ETFs.

As I write this in November 2008, municipal bonds are paying the highest yields I have seen in many years, so take advantage of them. I want to be clear: You never want to put money that is in an IRA, 401(k), or other tax-deferred account in municipals. Because your money is already tax-deferred, you get no added benefit from buying munis. So I am talking about money you invest outside of your IRA and 401(k). Now, I know that earlier I told you that the bond portion of your IRA and 401(k) should be kept in Treasuries with short maturities, but I have a different strategy for municipal bonds. I think it is smart to invest in municipal bonds with maturities of 10 to 20 years. As of November 2008, a 20-year general-obligation municipal bond has a yield of 5.14%. For someone in the 28% federal tax bracket, that is the equivalent of a 7.1% yield. That is a seriously great return on your money. If you are in a higher tax bracket, your return will be even higher.

As much as I love municipal bonds, I want to emphasize that this strategy only makes sense if you have at least $100,000 to invest; that is how much you need to be able to buy a diversified portfolio of five to 10 different bonds and not be hit with outrageous fees. (If you don't have that much money, stick with Treasury notes.)

Another strategy to generate more income in 2009 is to invest a portion of your money in high-dividend individual stocks or ETFs.

Because of the steep market losses, some company dividend payouts are now 5% or even higher. That's a lot better than what you can get at the bank.

However, you need to know that dividend stocks of course have greater risk than a bank CD. Even though you are receiving a nice steady dividend payout, the underlying value of your shares can indeed fall. And in today's tough economy, there is the possibility that some companies—such as the hard-pressed financial services industry—might find that they have to suspend or reduce their dividend payout. You need to understand that companies choose to pay dividends—they are not required to do so. In the third quarter of 2008, more than 100 companies cut their dividends, according to Standard & Poor's.

So here's my strategy for cautious dividend investing:

- **Invest only money that you know you will not need to cash in for at least the next 10 years. You will earn income (the dividend payout) on the money, but because these are stocks, you want to know that if the share price declines you won't have to sell at a big loss.**
- **Stick with low-cost ETFs. Owning individual stocks increases your risk of suffering big losses if there is an unexpected problem in that one company or industry. It's safer to invest in a di-**

versified portfolio of dividend-paying stocks. I like Vanguard High Dividend Yield (VYM) and iShares Select Dividend Index (DVY) if you invest in ETFs.

5

ACTION PLAN

Saving

The New Reality

Even safe havens can be risky during a credit crisis. The high-profile failure of IndyMac bank in July 2008 resulted in some depositors receiving an initial payment of just 50 cents on the dollar for money they had at the bank that exceeded Federal Deposit Insurance Corp. (FDIC) coverage. Another jolt came in September 2008 when the Reserve, a money market mutual fund company, announced that its Reserve Primary Fund "broke the buck." Money market mutual funds are designed to always maintain a fixed $1 value per share. Their sole purpose is to provide safe savings through a low yield. But one of the Reserve Primary Fund's investments was a Lehman Brothers security. When Lehman went under, so did the value of that security.

As I write this in November 2008, it is still not clear how much Reserve shareholders will receive when the fund is liquidated; it could be 97 cents on the dollar. Another disturbing development is that shareholders of 15 money market funds managed by the Reserve have had their accounts frozen for more than a month—meaning they have no access to money that is supposed to be in the most liquid of investment accounts.

The Reserve's problems triggered massive redemption requests from other money fund investors at other companies; in September, the Department of the Treasury had to step in and offer a temporary insurance fund to stop an all-out run on money market funds (more on this below).

The timing of the savings scare couldn't be worse. Never has having an emergency savings account been more important. The weak economy increases the odds that we will see rising layoffs in 2009; that's why I want you to push as hard as you can to find a way to set aside at least eight months of living expenses in an insured savings account. As I explained in "Action Plan: Credit," if you've slid by in the past thinking you could always tap your credit card in a pinch, that's not going to work this year. Credit lines are being reduced, and even if you have been spared so far, I have news for you: If you get laid off and start using your credit card more, you better believe the credit card company is going to think about cutting your credit limit the minute they catch wind that your unpaid balance keeps growing. Nor is your home equity line of credit (HELOC) a viable "emergency" fund anymore. If you still have an open HELOC, consider yourself lucky. With falling home prices eroding equity throughout 2007 and 2008, banks have been closing down HELOC accounts. And HELOC closures may continue in 2009 as many housing markets continue to struggle.

Bottom line: In 2009, everyone must have a safe standard savings account that will cover eight months of living costs. Rely on credit lines and HELOCs and you put your family at extreme risk.

What you must do in 2009

- **Make sure your bank or credit union is covered by federal deposit insurance.**
- **Check that what you have on deposit is eligible for full insurance coverage in the unlikely event your bank or credit union fails. Through December 31, 2009, the general limit has been raised to $250,000 from its previous $100,000, but you need to understand the ins and outs.**
- **If your savings is in a money market mutual fund sold through a brokerage or mutual fund firm, consider moving your money into the Treasury money market fund at that company.**
- **Build up your savings to cover eight months of living expenses.**

- Move all money you need within the next five to 10 years into savings. Money you need soon does not belong in the stock market.

Your 2009 Savings Action Plan

SITUATION: You don't know if your bank or credit union is backed by federal insurance.

ACTION: Confirm that your bank is part of the Federal Deposit Insurance Corp. (FDIC) program or that your credit union is part of the National Credit Union Administration's insurance fund (NCUA). You can check a recent statement or swing by the bank or credit union. If you see the FDIC or NCUA insurance logos displayed anywhere on a statement or front door, you are halfway home. Another option is to go to www.myfdicinsurance.gov or www.ncua.gov and use the online tools to confirm that where you save is indeed backed by federal insurance.

SITUATION: You don't know if all of your money on deposit at the bank or credit union is covered by insurance.

ACTION: Know the new insurance limits for 2009. Prior to the credit crisis, each individual had a base guarantee of up to $100,000 per bank. So if you had a checking account, a CD, and a money market, all the accounts were fully insured if their combined total did not exceed $100,000. If you had a joint account, you and the person you shared the account with were eligible for another $100,000 each of coverage. (The same limits applied for federally insured credit unions.)

For 2009, the limit for banks and credit unions has been raised to $250,000 per person per bank/credit union. The Treasury made this change in October 2008 to stave off a run on banks from depositors spooked by the continuing fallout from the credit crisis. If you have less than $250,000 at any single bank or credit union and that bank or credit union is federally insured, stop worrying. You are fine in 2009.

SITUATION: Given the new $250,000 limit, you want to know if it is smart to invest $250,000 in a high-rate five-year CD your bank is offering.

ACTION: No. You have to understand that currently the $250,000 insurance is good only through December 31, 2009. It may be renewed past 2009, but as of now, we do not know if it will be extended or made permanent in 2010. For now you have to act as if the limit will go back to $100,000 until you hear differently. So do not lock up $250,000 at one bank in case the limits are reduced; it might mean you could have $150,000 in uninsured money.

To be absolutely safe, limit the money you deposit at any one bank to $100,000 or stick with a CD that expires by December 31, 2009.

SITUATION: You already purchased a long-term CD for more than $100,000 and now you're worried about what will happen if the limits are rolled back after 2009.

ACTION: Don't do anything yet. I don't think you need to rush to make any changes. Check with your bank—or my Web site—by December to find out what's going to happen in 2010. If the limit is reduced to $100,000, you can still choose to cash in your CD early. Most banks will dock you with a penalty for an early withdrawal, but it is typically limited to forfeiting some of your interest, not principal. For now, sit tight and let's see what happens by the end of 2009.

WEB SITE ALERT: *You have my promise that the minute the FDIC and NCUA announce any changes in 2009, I will have an update at my Web site.*

SITUATION: You have more than $250,000 at one bank and are worried your money isn't 100% covered by FDIC insurance.

ACTION: You may still have full insurance coverage, but you need to check that your accounts meet the obscure rules that extend your insurance past the basic $250,000. The quickest and best way to make sure your accounts are fully insured is to go to www.myfdicinsurance.gov and plug your bank info into the easy-to-use calculator. In just a few simple steps you will have verification straight from the FDIC if all your accounts are fully insured. (Credit union members should use the NCUA Calculator at http://webapps.ncua.gov/ins/). If you don't have easy access to a computer, I recommend marching down to your bank or credit union and having them go online with you to verify the level of coverage you have; don't just take a teller's word for it. You want to see your account information plugged into the EDIE tool (at a bank) or the NCUA Calculator (for a credit union).

SITUATION: You worry that the FDIC or NCUA will run out of money if things get really bad and there are lots of failures. You fear the insurance really isn't going to be there if and when you need it.

ACTION: Rest assured your money is safe as long as it is covered by federal insurance. That insurance is backed by the full faith and credit of the United States government. Please don't get worked up if you hear or read ominous stories that the insurance funds are running short of money in 2009. I certainly hope that doesn't happen, and I am in no way suggesting that it will. But these are difficult times and there may be more bank failures or credit union failures if our economy and the credit markets continue to struggle. But here's the big picture to stay focused on: The FDIC and NCUA can go directly to the Treasury to get any money they need to fulfill their stated insurance promises. And the Treasury will raise any extra money it may need to cover losses that exceed what is already set aside in the insurance funds. There is absolutely no way our government is going to let depositors with insured accounts lose a penny. That promise is one of the pillars of our financial system.

SITUATION: You worry that if your bank or credit union fails, your account will be frozen and you won't be able to pay your bills or get cash out.

ACTION: Relax. Typically, when a bank or credit union is taken over by regulators it occurs on a Friday and by Monday everything is open and running as if nothing happened. It is in the best interests of the regulators to make sure depositors have quick access to their money. That's not only "good business," it is also how the regulators prevent a panicked run on the banks.

SITUATION: Your money is at a credit union and you are wondering if you should move it to an FDIC-insured bank.

ACTION: As long as your credit union belongs to the National Credit Administration's insurance fund (NCUA), your money is safe. The coverage limits and government backing are the same as those at an FDIC-insured bank. There is no need to move your money.

SITUATION: You have money deposited with an online bank and wonder if it is safe.

ACTION: Check if the online bank says it is part of the FDIC insurance program. Every bank that is in the FDIC insurance program—whether online or "bricks and mortar"—is safe. You can check the home page of your online bank; all banks that participate in the program will advertise that fact boldly. But I think it is smart to double-check directly with the FDIC; go to www.myfdicinsurance.gov to verify you are protected, and confirm that every penny is in fact insured.

SITUATION: A stock mutual fund you bought at your bank had a big loss in 2008. The bank is FDIC insured, so you thought your money is safe.

ACTION: You need to understand that FDIC insurance does not cover investments, such as a stock fund. Federal insurance for banks and for credit unions covers deposit accounts, not investment accounts. A deposit account can be a checking, savings, CD, or money market account. But banks are also allowed to sell investments. Mutual funds are investments. Stocks and exchange-traded funds (ETFs) you buy through a bank are investments. And they have zero insurance. Zero. When you opened the account you probably signed some sort of acknowledgment that you understood this, but those disclosures are easy to miss. And, of course, there was no guarantee that your friendly bank account manager who was excited to have you make the investment took the time to slowly and clearly spell things out.

When you invest in the stock market—whether it be through a fund you buy at a bank, a credit union, a brokerage, or a fund company—you have no protection against bear market losses.

SITUATION: Last time I checked, my savings account had an interest rate of 5%, but now it is below 2.5%. Should I move to a bank offering accounts with higher yields?

ACTION: It is always smart to shop around for the best-yielding savings accounts, but you need to understand that 2008 was the year of the falling bank rate. Banks peg the savings rate they offer consumers to the Federal Reserve's Federal Funds Rate. And for more than a year the Federal Reserve has been aggressively cutting the Federal Funds Rate. In December 2007, the rate was at 4.25%. In

November 2008, it was down to 1%, and as I write, there is talk that it may go down to 0%. So if you are earning more than 1% or so on a regular savings account, that's actually pretty good. I am all for moving your money to the highest-yielding bank accounts, and you can check Web sites such as www.bankrate.com for banks that offer the highest savings rates. But if you have a competitive yield right where you are and it is FDIC insured, I wouldn't make it a huge priority in 2009 to hunt for an extra 0.25% in yield. But hey, if you have the time and energy to shop around, go for it. Just remember: Only put your money in a bank that is FDIC insured or a federally insured credit union.

SITUATION: Your savings are in a money market mutual fund your broker told you was safe, but you wonder if it's as safe as an account at an FDIC-insured bank.

ACTION: The short answer is no. A money market mutual fund (MMMF) sold by a brokerage firm or a mutual fund firm is not backed by permanent federal insurance. Only a money market deposit account (MMDA) sold through a federally insured bank or credit union, or a bank subsidiary of a brokerage or mutual fund company, is eligible for insurance.

I know, I know: MMDA, MMMF—why do they have to make it all so confusing?

So just to be sure you have it down straight:

MMDA: *Sold at a bank or credit union, or through a bank subsidiary of a brokerage or fund company. Eligible for federal deposit insurance.*

MMMF: *Sold through a brokerage firm or mutual fund company. No insurance.*

Now, in normal times, an MMMF is considered just as safe as an MMDA. But I don't have to tell you how *not* normal the times are for us right now.

And I don't think you should rest easy with the temporary insurance offered by the emergency Treasury action last September. It's important to understand that this Treasury plan is temporary and voluntary. We don't know how long the Treasury will keep offering this deal to MMMFs; Treasury is currently authorized to keep the plan through September 18, 2009, but it must reauthorize the plan every three months between now and then. Your brokerage firm or mutual fund firm must choose to become part of the program (and pay a fee to participate). So, at the very least, you need to check with your brokerage or fund firm to find out if it is participating in this temporary insurance program. But here's the really important caveat: Only deposits in MMMFs as of the close of business September 19, 2008, are eligible for the Treasury's insurance.

That's just too many question marks to deal with if you ask me. Here's my safe and sound MMMF strategy for 2009: Keep your money with the same firm but move it into the Treasury MMMF (every major brokerage and fund company has this option). If your money is invested in U.S. Treasuries, you have nothing to worry about. Your money is backed by the full faith and credit of the U.S. government. There aren't going to be any defaults in that portfolio. And you don't have to worry if the Treasury Department eventually removes its current MMMF insurance offer. If you don't have a Treasury MMMF option at your existing brokerage or fund company, then I would consider moving my money into an insured bank deposit in 2009, or to a brokerage or fund company that offers a Treasury MMMF. (To be extra safe, I recommend that money you need to pay bills, etc., be moved into a bank or credit union MMDA account. We've seen how the Reserve had to temporarily freeze some accounts; you need to make sure that money you need quick access to is in fact available. Right now the only way to ensure ready access is with an insured bank or credit union account.)

SITUATION: You understand why it makes sense to have eight months of living expenses set aside in an emergency savings fund, but there is no way you can ever save that much.

ACTION: I am well aware how stretched you are financially. I fully expect that many of you may not be able to flip the switch and magically have a bank account that is stuffed with enough money to cover eight months of living expenses. But you must start moving toward that goal. Month by month you must build security for yourself and your family. You may get to the eight-month goal in six months of aggressive saving, or it may take you a few years. That's okay. The point is that you are moving in the right direction. Every month you will have more security, not less. Check out "Action Plan: Spending" for steps on how to reduce your expenses so you have more money to put toward goals such as this one.

One of the best ways to get on a consistent savings pattern is to set up an automated deposit from your checking account into a savings account. Studies show that once you automate you tend to stick with it; that's true of bank savings accounts and your 401(k) investing. As the saying goes, set it and forget it.

Now, how much should you have deposited each month? Here's the goal for 2009. Decide how much you can afford to deposit. Now add 20% to that amount. Don't cheat here. If you were going to set aside $100 a month, commit to $120. If you were going to aim for $500 a month, it's now $600 a month. Will that be hard? Yes. Will it take some serious spending cuts? Probably. But in 2009 you cannot afford to be laid back and do what is easy. You must push yourself as hard as possible to build your security as quickly as possible.

SITUATION: You are retired and need safe income, but you can't live off of 2.5% interest in your bank CDs. What are you supposed to do?

ACTION: Keep some of your money in the bank; no matter how low the yield—safety first. I know the current market is especially hard for retirees who depend on interest income from their bank deposits to help cover their monthly living costs. Yields on savings accounts have dwindled as the Federal Reserve aggressively lowered its Federal Funds Rate from above 4% in late 2007 to just over 1.0% in late 2008. During the same stretch, the cost of everything rose. The official inflation rate hovered around 4% in 2008, but out in the real world, the price of basic necessities—food, medications—increased at more than twice that official rate of inflation. I don't have a lot of cheery news for savers in 2009. Though long-term bank rates will rise, that may not happen in 2009, as the Federal Reserve may be more preoccupied with keeping rates low to deal with a stuck credit market and an economy in recession.

That said, you must keep your savings safe, no matter how low the yield. Some relief is on the way in 2009, as Social Security benefits increased 6.2% over what you received in 2008. That is the largest inflation adjustment since 1982. I also recommend checking out municipal bonds; as I write, you can get yields of nearly 5% on bonds with fifteen-year maturities. That's a good deal right now and it does not require you take on the risk of investing in longer-term issues. And please check out my dividend stock strategy in "Action Plan: Retirement Investing." It may be a smart way for you to earn more income on a small portion of your money that you're comfortable investing in the stock market.

SITUATION: You have a mortgage or a car loan with a bank that failed and you wonder if you need to keep paying it.

ACTION: You must keep paying. A bank's failure does not excuse you from paying your loan.

Very soon after a bank failure, you should receive notice of the bank that has taken over your account. And if all goes well, you will just keep paying exactly as you have, with no disruption. Now, that said, I want you to keep very careful records of all your payments. If you use online banking, print out each payment for at least six months and tuck them away in a safe place. As I said, the transition should be seamless, but when Bank A takes over Bank B, sometimes the wires can get crossed in the back office during the switchover. So you want to have perfect records to prove any problem is not because you fell behind on payments. If you do receive a notice that you haven't paid, you have to not only deal with the bank but check your credit reports (go to www.annualcreditreport.com; you are entitled to one free credit report a year from each of the three credit bureaus) to make sure the bank has not mistakenly reported your loan payment as late or delinquent. If it is showing up on your report, you must ride the bank hard to correct the mistake. At the same time, file a dispute with the credit bureau. By law, they must look into the matter and report back to you within 30 days. Don't take anyone's word that they will take care of it. You must stay on top of the issue and keep checking (and nudging) to make sure any mistake is cleared up. As I discussed in "Action Plan: Credit," 2009 is not a time to let your FICO credit score drop. Especially when your bank is the one that has tripped up.

6

ACTION PLAN

Spending

The New Reality

The financial crisis has served as a deafening wake-up call that will not stop ringing in your ears. You know in the very core of your being that you need to change how you run your financial life. There's no room anymore for just getting by or putting off the hard decisions for tomorrow. Tomorrow is here, and it requires a commitment to taking the actions that put you and your family on a lasting path to financial security.

You know you need to pay down your credit card debt to keep your credit line intact and your FICO score strong. You also know you can't rely on having easy access to a large credit card limit or HELOC in 2009 to cover emergency expenses. You know—or I hope you're at least beginning to realize—that you must come up with cash to put in a savings account for emergency protection. You have also woken up to the notion that you can't rely on huge home-price appreciation as your de facto retirement account. You know you must contribute more to your retirement savings because now is actually a great time to be investing for the long term.

There's only one problem. You don't know where you will come up with the money for all this.

The truth is that the most effective cash-generating action you need to take in 2009 is to *spend less*. The less you spend, the more money you will have after paying the monthly bills to put toward reducing your credit card debt, building your emergency savings, and increasing your retirement investing. It's not a news flash; it's just a fact.

This year is all about making more by spending less.

What you must do in 2009

- **Separate wants from needs.**
- **Get over your guilt that you aren't "providing" for your kids.**
- **Strike the word "deserve" from the conversation. What you deserve is irrelevant; what you can truly afford is all that counts.**
- **Try to negotiate better terms on a car loan you can't keep up with.**
- **Be very careful when asked to cosign any loan, no matter how much you love the person who is asking for your help.**

Your 2009 Spending Action Plan

SITUATION: You know your family needs to save more, but you have no idea where to start.

ACTION: Get a grip on where your money is going. You can't move forward building an honest financial life if you don't first understand where you are today. I want you to slowly and carefully fill out the Household Cash Flow worksheet below. To do this, you need to first pull out a year's worth of bank statements and credit card statements. The amount you put in the right-hand column should be the average cost for the past 12 months.

WEB SITE ALERT: *A more extensive version of this worksheet is available for download on www.suzeorman.com.*

EXPENSES	MONTHLY COST
HOME	
MORTGAGE/RENT	
HOME EQUITY LOAN	
PROPERTY TAX	
INSURANCE	
MAINTENANCE	
UTILITIES	
Gas and Electric	

EXPENSES	MONTHLY COST
Heating	
Water	
Home Phone	
Cell Phone	
Cable/TV	
Internet	
MAINTENANCE	
Repairs/Upgrades	
Gardener	
Snow Removal	
TOTAL MONTHLY HOME EXPENSES:	________
FOOD	
Groceries	
Dining Out/Takeout	
Coffee	
TOTAL FOOD:	________
CAR/TRANSPORTATION	
Car Loan #1	
Car Loan #2	
Gas	
Maintenance	
Tolls/Paid Parking	
Car Insurance (total all cars)	

EXPENSES	MONTHLY COST
Public Transportation	
TOTAL CAR COSTS:	______
OTHER INSURANCE	
Health Insurance*	
Life Insurance*	
Disability Insurance*	
Long-Term-Care Insurance*	
Dental Insurance*	
TOTAL OTHER COSTS:	______
MISC. SPENDING	
Child Care	
Private School Tuition	
Entertainment (Movies, DVD rentals, Concerts, Sporting Events)	
Hair/Manicures/Pedicures	
Club Memberships	
Computer Equipment and Games	
Clothes	
Gifts	
Vacations	
Medical Copays and Out-of-Pocket Expenses	
Pet (Food and Vet)	
Media Subscriptions (Newspapers, Magazines, Online)	

EXPENSES	MONTHLY COST
Charitable Contributions	
Other	
Other	
Other	
TOTAL MISC. SPENDING:	______
OTHER LOANS/DEBT	
Credit Card 1	
Credit Card 2	
Credit Card 3	
Student Loan	
401(k) Loan	
Bank/Personal Loan	
TOTAL OTHER DEBTS:	______
MONTHLY SAVINGS/TAX PAYMENTS	
Emergency Savings Account	
401(k) Contribution*	
IRA Contribution	
College Savings Fund	
Self-Employment Tax Payments	
TOTAL SAVINGS/TAX PAYMENTS:	______
TOTAL EXPENSES (A):	______

*If these items are taken out of your paycheck, they do not need to be itemized on this worksheet, which tallies expenses against take-home pay.

INCOME	MONTHLY AMT.
After-Tax Pay	
Rental Income	
Dividend/Interest Income	
Social Security	
Retirement Income (401(k), IRA, and Pension)	
TOTAL INCOME (B):	________
TOTAL INCOME–TOTAL EXPENSES (B–A):	________

SITUATION: Your expenses are more than your income.

ACTION: Circle every expense in your worksheet that is a "want." It is imperative to separate expenses that are for true needs (health insurance, the electricity bill) from those that are not crucial for your family to function (gym membership, new clothes, computer games, etc.).

If you do not have an eight-month emergency savings fund, if you have credit card debt, and if you are not saving for retirement, you have no choice but to reduce and even eliminate many of the "wants" your family is spending money on.

This is not supposed to be a comfortable or easy exercise. Cutting down from four manicures a month to three is not going to get you where you need to go. Your financial security is buried in those expenses. The more you are willing to curtail spending on those expenses, the more money you have to protect your family. The $25 you don't mindlessly shell out to the kids every week when they head out to spend time with friends is $100 a month you have to put toward a term life insurance policy that protects them if anything were to happen to you. The $300 a month you don't spend on the second (or third) car your family can do without is your future retirement security; put that much in a Roth IRA for 20 years and you will have more than $157,000, assuming your money grows at an annualized 7% rate.

SITUATION: You feel guilty cutting back on what you've always provided for your family.

ACTION: Decide once and for all if you want to indulge or protect your family.

It really is that simple. If you have credit card debt and no emergency savings, I have to tell you, you do not care about your family's safety and security. All you care about is being the hero who doesn't say no, the bottomless ATM for every desire, expectation, and wish your family has.

That is indulgent. And destructive. Let's walk through this together. You look at your expense and income worksheet, get frustrated, and decide to just continue down the path of overspending. You ignore the fact that your credit card balance keeps rising. You ignore the fact that you have no emergency savings. You ignore the fact that you have very little saved up for retirement. You ignore the fact that you don't have health insurance because it is just too expensive.

And then you get laid off. Or you get sick. You can't pay the mortgage, and you have no savings to help you in this time of emergency. So the downward spiral begins. You might even lose your home. All because you feel as if you must always give your kids everything they want—and right now. How does that indulge your kids?

Or let's look even further into the future. Twenty years from now, your little ones are going to be adults, working to make ends meet for their own families. Then you come knocking on the door saying you can't afford to support yourself in retirement because you never saved up enough during your prime working years, the years when you made the decision to give your kids everything they wanted. How does that indulge your adult kids?

I appreciate that it may initially be hard to institute new financial priorities and habits in your family. Change is always a process that takes getting used to. But the real problem here is that you think acting responsibly with your money will be punishment for your kids. You think that by slowing down the spending you are taking something away from them. I couldn't disagree more. I see it as protecting them. When you make the commitment to spend less, you will have more money to put toward what your family needs: lasting financial security.

And I have to tell you: How receptive will your kids be to the change comes down to how you sell it. If you are moping, if they can feel your guilt, they are going to feel lousy. Your kids don't deserve that.

Children are incredibly adaptable, and they are going to take their cues from you. So don't pitch this as a scary time and don't suggest that they are in any way to blame for your problems. In an age-appropriate manner, let them know that you are all going to be fine, but you need to be extra careful with spending and saving to make sure the family is safe during these challenging times.

SITUATION: Even after removing the "wants," you still don't have money to put toward paying off your credit card debt and building savings.

ACTION: Look for ways to pay less for your needs. You need a phone, but do you need a home phone and a cell phone? Does your family need the super-deluxe cell plan that lets everyone aimlessly text to their heart's delight, or might you be able to spend $50 less a month with a scaled-back plan? Have you really, seriously done everything to reduce your utility bills? I am talking about the low-hanging fruit of inexpensive insulation, unplugging unused electronics, replacing burned-out bulbs with energy-efficient CFLs. I know you have heard all of this before. But you sort of filed it away under "someday I really should." That day is here. I bet you can reduce what you spend on your family's needs by 10% to 20% if you put your heart into it.

Insure Big Savings

Health insurance, car insurance, and home insurance (including renter's insurance) are three of the most important "needs" for every family. Without question, they are necessary expenses. But there are great ways to lower your insurance premiums. You are not to reduce your level of coverage, but rather, make sure you have taken advantage of every deal and discount possible.

- Raise your deductibles on all your policies. You can save 10% or more if you agree to a deductible of $500 or $1,000 rather than just $250. There's no need to keep a low deductible when you have a solid emergency savings fund that can cover any out-of-pocket expenses.
- Keep your auto and homeowner's/renter policies with one insurance company. You will be eligible for a 10%–20% "multiline" discount.

- Designate one car as your "low mileage" car; if you keep annual mileage below 7,500–10,000 miles, the premium discount can be 10% or so.
- Keep your FICO credit score above 700. Some insurers base the premium rate you are offered on your credit score. The higher your score, the more likely you are to get the best terms on all your insurance.

SITUATION: Three years ago, you and your partner agreed you would be a stay-at-home mom, but your partner's commission-based salary has fallen along with the bad economy, so you are stuck putting some expenses on your credit card, knowing you will not be able to pay it off in full.

ACTION: Base your financial decisions on what you have today, not what you had in the past. If your family can no longer afford to live on one income, you must consider going back to work.

I say that with great understanding of how hard this will be for you to consider. But remember, 2009 is about making the right and honest choices to build a secure future. And what is right is not always the same as what is easy. Going back to work when you believe it is far more important to be a stay-at-home parent is an emotionally charged and difficult step to contemplate, but in these tough times, it just might be necessary.

You need to focus on what is best for your children. I believe very strongly that financial security is what's best for your children. And if you cannot honestly keep your family financially secure—by being out of credit card debt, having a hefty savings fund, and keeping your retirement savings on track—you are not doing what is best for them.

Start by considering whether you (or your partner) can take on part-time work to supplement what is coming in from the one income. That may be a way to make more without having to rely completely on child care. But if that doesn't close the gap, you must think about taking on a bigger job. If it needs to be full-time, it needs to be full-time. Maybe not forever, but for now. 2009: the year you take action to build financial security for your family.

SITUATION: You can't afford to pay private-school tuition and invest the maximum in your retirement accounts.

ACTION: It might be time to rethink whether public school is the better move for your entire family. Look, I know this is a huge issue, and I am not suggesting you make a decision in the next 15 minutes about whether you can continue to send your 10-year-old to private school. But I also think it is shortsighted to presume that this expense is untouchable. If you are shortchanging your retirement savings, or if your emergency fund is nonexistent, you really need to think through whether you are doing the best for your child. If your issue is that you do not think your local public schools provide the quality education you want for your children, I want you to take a deep breath and consider moving to a community with a strong public school system. As I said, this is not a quick or easy decision. And to be honest, 2009 is probably not the best time to try to sell your home. But I encourage you to at least start giving this serious consideration. Will home values and property taxes be higher in a town with high-quality schools? Probably. But I seriously doubt it will cost you the $30,000 or more a year it can take to send two children to private school.

SITUATION: You lost your job and can no longer afford to make the payments on your family's second car, but you owe more on the loan than you can get at trade-in.

ACTION: Call up your lender and see if you can get the loan terms modified. Ideally, you don't want to extend the length of the loan (that will increase your total cost over the life of the loan), but push to see if you can get the interest rate reduced. That will lower your costs. Or perhaps the lender will agree to a temporary period of reduced payments.

There's a good chance lenders will be receptive to playing "Let's Make a New Deal." The financial and credit crisis has been devastating for car lenders. Their lots are already filled with repossessed cars—overflowing, in fact. At the same time, the credit crunch has made it much harder for potential buyers to get car loans for new cars. That has caused a massive decline in sales that has jam-packed the same lot already stuffed with repos, with new cars that aren't selling. This is a car dealer's worst nightmare, so that increases the chance the lender may be willing to work out a deal to keep your car off his lot. Getting a reduced payment from you is better than no payment—especially if it means one less car on the lot.

SITUATION: You just want your car to be repossessed already—you're sick of trying to keep up with the payments.

ACTION: If you know you can't afford the car, hand the car back to the lender rather than waiting for repossession. By proactively contacting the lender and giving the car back, you will avoid paying fees charged for repossession. And more important, you will avoid the trauma of having your car towed away from your work or home. You change the dynamic by making an embarrassing act into an act of responsibility.

SITUATION: You turned the car back in—or it was repossessed—but you were told you still owed the lender money.

ACTION: You are responsible for the difference between what you still owed on the loan and what the lender can recoup by reselling the car. If you can't cover that payment, you did not live up to your financial obligation. Whether you turned in the car or it was formally repossessed, failure to pay the balance will stay on your credit report for seven years.

SITUATION: You want to borrow from your 401(k) to keep up with the car payments.

ACTION: Do not touch your retirement savings. If you need to keep the car or you want to avoid having a repossession on your credit report, you must find other income sources to make the payment. Go back and review the Household Cash Flow worksheet at the beginning of this chapter. If you need more cash, find it from spending less. The absolute worst move you can make is to pull money out of your 401(k). As I explain in detail in "Action Plan: Retirement Investing," it is never wise to touch your retirement savings. And in 2009 it is downright dangerous, given the increased possibility of being laid off. Lose your job and your 401(k) loan will need to be repaid within a few months. Where are you going to come up with that money?

SITUATION: **Your eldest child heads to college in 2010 and you're feeling like this is the last chance to take a long family vacation, even though it probably means putting $4,000 on your credit card that you won't be able to pay off immediately.**

ACTION: You will get no argument from me that family time is a high priority. As you may have heard me say, my mantra is "People First, Then Money, Then Things." But that doesn't translate to giving you carte blanche to spend whatever you want to create those memories. They are not priceless memories. If you need to run up credit card debt to finance the memories, they have a very steep cost: a 15% interest rate, on average.

This is not about what you and your family deserve. We all deserve vacations. But you have to face up to what is going on in our economy right now. I am not a pessimist; we will eventually move past this financial mess. But in the interim, what you and your family need is to be safe. An unpaid credit card balance is not safe. Not having an emergency savings fund is not safe. Same goes for no retirement savings. If you haven't taken care of those priorities, you can't afford to take an expensive vacation. Period. That doesn't mean you can't spend time with your family and create lasting memories. Take the vacation—just do it at home, or closer to home, this year.

SITUATION: Your daughter is getting married. You have all dreamed of a big wedding, but your investments took a big hit last year and the only way you can afford the wedding is to put it on your credit card. This is a once-in-a-lifetime event, so it's not like you can just say no.

ACTION: You can, and must, say no. It is absolutely unacceptable to take on any sort of debt to pay for a wedding. No exceptions. I don't care what anyone dreamed of.

Do you deep down, *honestly*, believe that what you spend is a reflection of your love for your daughter? Do you honestly believe that it is better to take on $20,000 in credit card debt to impress your friends, rather than use that $20,000 for retirement savings? Step back for a moment and put this decision to the Need vs. Want test. What you and your daughter *want* is a big expensive wedding. But all that is really *needed* is an affordable wedding that is full of love.

SITUATION: You love giving gifts. It is important to you and something your friends and family have come to expect from you. You can't imagine stopping your gift-giving ways just to have more to save for yourself.

ACTION: As wonderful as it is that you give gifts, you and I both know that your friends and family don't love you because of the gifts. If you have yet to build an emergency savings fund that can cover eight months of living costs, you must curtail your gift giving so you can give yourself something far more important: security.

Besides, you are never, ever to buy gifts that you can't afford to pay for immediately. As I explained in "Action Plan: Credit," an unpaid credit card balance in 2009 puts you at great risk of falling into a costly vicious cycle you will find it hard to climb out of. Worried what your friends and family will think if they don't receive an expensive gift this year? Come on. Do you really think anyone who cares about you would feel good if they received a gift with an unspoken price tag that said, *This gift cost $50 that I couldn't afford and means I will not be able to pay off my credit card bill this month*?

SITUATION: You are struggling to make ends meet, but you don't want to stop contributing to the charities you have supported in the past.

ACTION: Can you give time rather than money this year? I understand how important it is to help those in need. But you have important needs this year too. And it is not selfish to make your financial safety and security a priority. If you need to reduce or suspend your contributions this year to shore up your finances, that's the right and honest move for you to make.

I realize how hard this is, especially when charities are also feeling the pinch and are stepping up their requests for donations. But you must give only what you can honestly afford. If that means no financial contributions in 2009, that is okay. I encourage you to donate your time—or more of your time than you already give—to the causes you support. That is a valuable contribution. And to be honest, I think it can also have a great unintended benefit for you: In these very scary times, it can be calming to focus on what you can do through your actions to make the world a better place.

Now, that said, I also know how upsetting it can be to curtail helping others in need. Take another hard look at the Household Cash Flow worksheet and see if there are any costs you could pare back to free up a little money to contribute to the causes most important to you. Challenge yourself: "I want to cut $X a month in savings so I can continue to make charitable contributions in 2009." Often, having a specific goal makes it easier to focus on "wants" that you can do without. If only for 2009.

SITUATION: Your son graduates from college in a few months and needs a car for work. He has asked you to cosign for a car loan.

ACTION: If you cannot cover the payments yourself, then you are never to cosign a loan. You need to understand that cosigning makes you legally responsible for the loan; in the event your child can't make the payment, you are expected to come up with the payment. Failure to do so will hurt your FICO score, not just your child's.

And let me define what it means to be able to afford to cosign: You have no credit card debt yourself. You are not struggling to make your mortgage and car payments. Even if you can afford to cover the payments, I want you to carefully consider what you are doing. If your child can't get a car loan on his own, you need to ask yourself why. Is he buying an expensive car when his budget can afford only a moderate-priced car? Is he focusing only on new cars for their "wow" factor, rather than buying a safe, reliable older car that is more affordable? Is there something the lender knows about his credit score that you don't—such as the fact that he is already up to his ears in credit card debt? Helping a child who is just getting started is fine, but helping a child who has already abused credit and has no clue how to be financially responsible is not acceptable.

If you decide to go ahead and cosign, I recommend that you be in charge of making the payment. I have seen too many parents cosign and assume their kid is making the payments, only to get a disturbing letter from the lender that the loan is delinquent and everyone's FICO score has been hurt. I know you are focused on your kid being an independent adult, but if he or she needs your help with a loan, you have every right to oversee the payment.

SITUATION: You need a new car, but you don't want to overreach and end up like your neighbor who had her car repossessed last year.

ACTION: Find out what you can afford with a maximum loan term of three years. That's what you can afford. It makes no financial sense to stretch into a more expensive car if you need to extend the loan term to four or five years. That's a colossal waste of money. What you need to understand is that a car is a lousy investment. It is guaranteed to lose money; the trade-in value will never cover the purchase price or the interest payments on a loan. Therefore, you want to keep your cost as low as possible by limiting yourself to a three-year loan. At www.bankrate.com, you can see what typical car rates are in your area and use the free calculator to figure out your monthly costs.

And I want to be clear, I am talking about a regular loan. No leases. Not now, not ever. With a car loan, you will eventually own the car free and clear and can drive it for five to seven more years without having to worry about your monthly payment. If you lease, you typically fall into a trap where you just keep rolling over into a new lease every three years. So you are always making payments. Given that we just discussed what a lousy investment a car is, why would you ever choose a never-ending cycle of car payments?

Before you start shopping, make sure your FICO credit score is at least 720. There are indeed great deals to be had given all the unsold and repossessed cars on dealer lots, but you need to have a high credit score to get a loan with a reasonable rate. In a slowing economy, where lenders are downright scared to lend, they are going to offer reasonable deals only to borrowers with sparkling credit. In November 2008, a FICO score of 720 or better would make you eligible for a 6.7% car loan rate. If your score was 620–660, the rate was 12%.

I also recommend taking a look at certified preowned cars; these are used cars that come with a limited warranty. Make sure the warranty is from the manufacturer, not the dealership. Given the huge inventory of repossessed cars, you may be able to find an especially good deal on a used car. Sure, right now you might also be able to score a great deal on a new car if you have a solid FICO score. But please remember that the goal is to spend the least amount of money for a car that is safe and meets your commuting needs.

SILVER LINING: *The federal sales-tax deduction is reinstated for the 2008 and 2009 tax years. As part of the big $700 billion bailout bill, Congress reinstated an expired tax break that gives you the option of deducting either your state income tax or the sales tax you paid for the year. For residents of states with no (or low) personal income-tax rates who made big-ticket purchases, you can save money on your federal return if you itemize and claim the sales-tax deduction.*

A Pledge for 2009

Throughout this book I have asked you in various ways to change your actions, to think before acting, to act in a manner that might go against your instincts. I'm a firm believer that action is often the only antidote for overcoming fear or doubt, for burning through confusion, and for changing habits that have become ingrained patterns in our lives.

To that end, I am asking you to make the following pledge.

Within a month of reading this book, I ask that you:

- Do not spend money for one day
- Do not use your credit card for one week
- Do not eat out at a restaurant for one month

I think you will be surprised by the changes these resolutions bring about in you. In my own life I have found that small, mindful acts can change your entire worldview. Once you have fulfilled these three requests, I ask that you make a promise to yourself to make it your absolute priority to eliminate your outstanding credit card debt as soon as possible. What may have once seemed overwhelming and impossible, may suddenly seem like the right thing to do—a very necessary action to take—in 2009.

7

ACTION PLAN

Real Estate

The New Reality

Fallout from the mortgage crisis has affected every home in America. This is no longer a problem confined to the subprime market of reckless borrowers and the irresponsible lenders who egged them on. No one was left untouched.

Even if you have a mortgage you can afford and a home you love, the fact is your home is likely worth less than it was just a few years ago, and that puts a huge crimp in your financial planning. You convinced yourself that your home would continue to appreciate at a double-digit annual rate forever, with no possible downside. You baked those high values into your future financial plans and that made you feel richer than you actually were. But your bubble-induced sense of security led you to spend more and save less because you were so sure your mountain of home equity would pay for retirement or the kids' college tuition or the new room addition.

But it isn't playing out the way you imagined. Home values have plummeted back to 2004 levels and are still falling as I write this in November 2008. Suddenly, you must face the fact that your home is not going to fund all those capital expenses you were planning. That not only affects your long-term outlook, it could also endanger your short-term security. The newest housing trend sweeping the country is banks rescinding home equity lines of credit because falling home values make those open credit lines too risky. Any family that has relied on a HELOC as an emergency cash fund could be in trouble in 2009; your bank may remove your safety net.

And let's face it, 2009 is shaping up to be the worst year in decades to sell a home, even if you have equity. There is a 10-month backlog of homes on the market; that's more than double the level five years ago. A flood of bank-foreclosed homes, or homes up for a short sale (when what your home sells for is less than your remaining mortgage balance, and the bank forgives the difference), are a big factor in the market glut, but so is the frozen lending market. Banks do not want to lend money right now; the only borrowers they will even consider must jump through the highest qualifying hoops in more than a decade. That reduces the pool of prospective buyers of your home—including buyers who must turn around and sell their home in the same frozen market.

Renters are not immune either. Tens of thousands of renters have been kicked out of their homes since 2007 as their landlords fell behind on their mortgage payments and the bank foreclosed on the property. These were renters who wrote the check on time every month and had no clue that their home was at risk until they had an official note tacked to the front door telling them they had 30 days to vacate.

There will be no magical turnaround in 2009. The best we can hope for is a slowing of homes that fall into foreclosure. I have a moral problem with bailing out homeowners and lenders who had no right to do the deals they did. I certainly do not support a bailout of people who bought a home that was never affordable under any rational assessment, but I do think we are obliged to help those who, with moderate assistance today, can afford to stay in their home. Keeping those homeowners in their homes is the most effective way to stabilize the housing market. And let's be clear: There will be no widespread stabilization in our financial markets until the housing markets stabilize; home foreclosures are the epicenter of the credit crisis.

As I write, some major lenders have finally stepped up their effort to modify loans for some homeowners. And I expect we will see more and greater effort by lenders and the federal government to slow down the pace of foreclosures in 2009. Still, we should all expect that this year will continue to be a very tough time for real estate.

WEB SITE ALERT: *This book went to press in November 2008. I will post updated information on my Web site throughout the year whenever there are new mortgage-relief programs to share with you. Go to www.suzeorman.com.*

What you need to do in 2009

- Push for a "mortgage modification" if your current loan is too expensive.
- Do not use credit cards or retirement funds to pay for a too-expensive home.
- Stay informed about new programs, from lenders and the government, in the months ahead that aim to keep more homeowners out of foreclosure.
- Build a real savings fund; a HELOC should not be your safety net in 2009.
- Focus on your home's long-term value, not its price change from month to month.

Your 2009 Real Estate Action Plan

SITUATION: You can't afford the cost of your adjustable rate mortgage (ARM) since it reset, but you don't know what your options are.

ACTION: Start by contacting your lender and asking if there is any chance you can renegotiate (modify) your mortgage so your payments are more affordable. Please do this as soon as you think you're in trouble—over half of those whose homes are foreclosed never speak to their lender prior to foreclosure, according to the National Foundation for Consumer Credit Counseling (NFCC). This was far from easy throughout most of 2008, but as the severity of the crisis deepened, some lenders stepped up their willingness to modify loans for borrowers they deemed could afford their homes with a moderate level of assistance. When you call, right away ask for a loan-mitigation or workout specialist. Be prepared to document your financial hardship as well as your ability to afford the modified loan. You can get advice about how to talk to your lender at www.hud.gov. Click on "Guide to Avoiding Foreclosure." Better yet, the NFCC has HUD-approved housing counselors who can advise you and will act as an advocate with your lender for the best resolution for your situation. Call 866-557-2227—you'll be automatically connected to the agency closest to you—or visit their Homeowner Crisis Resource Center at www.housinghelpnow.org.

SITUATION: You contacted your lender five months ago and were told there was no way the lender would modify your loan to make it more affordable.

ACTION: Try again. Lenders who were saying no for a long time are now softening up and agreeing to modify loans. To be honest, this may be your best shot, rather than the government programs in their current forms. In October 2008, Bank of America announced an agreement with a group of state attorneys general to modify up to 400,000 subprime mortgages the bank acquired when it bought Countrywide earlier in the year. Also in October, JP Morgan Chase announced its intention to modify as many as 400,000 mortgages to more affordable terms in an effort to reduce foreclosures. And in mid-November, Citigroup had announced it was halting the foreclosure process for loans in its portfolio and would try to modify terms for as many as 500,000 of its distressed borrowers.

WEB SITE ALERT: *I anticipate we will see more lender and government programs in 2009 to slow down the pace of foreclosures; visit www.suzeorman.com for up-to-date information.*

SITUATION: The banks and Wall Street are getting help, but what programs exist to help homeowners?

ACTION: First of all, contact your lender; they are best equipped to tell you what assistance you may be eligible for. The pace of lenders offering their own programs is picking up (though the banks were woefully slow to offer such assistance through much of 2008).

You are supposed to be able to get government assistance sizing up whether you are a good candidate for a mortgage modification by calling the Hope Now alliance coordinated by the Department of Housing and Urban Development. Call 888-995-HOPE, or get more information at www.hopenow.com. Be prepared to be patient; though you can reach a live operator with ease, you may be told there is no counselor available and that you will need to call back later. And don't expect miracles; this is merely to help you size up your situation. Moreover, if the Hope Now counselor can't ascertain who actually owns your mortgage—an all-too-common problem given the millions of mortgages that were packaged with other mortgages and sold off as securities—you aren't going to be able to get past first base.

Given that lenders have been less than impressive in stepping up to the plate to help people stay in their homes, I want you to know what federal programs are available. But please be aware that these programs—limited and late in coming—may change in both scope and detail once the new administration is in place. Adding to the uncertainty is the problem of consumers whose loans, many of them subprime, have been sold in packages to outside investors worldwide; there is still disagreement over whether mortgages sold into these pools can be modified. With such a fluid and evolving situation, please periodically check my Web site for updates on the changes: www.suzeorman.com.

Here are the programs in place as of mid-November 2008:

The original FHASecure program, launched in August 2007, was limited to helping homeowners with good credit (translation: not subprime) refinance into a fixed-rate mortgage if they would be unable to keep up with the reset of their ARMs. The one big catch was that you couldn't already be behind in your mortgage payments, thereby shutting out the very people in need of help.

In July 2008, Congress passed the Housing and Economic Recovery Act, which effectively made FHASecure a viable option for subprime borrowers too. You can be eligible for a mortgage refinance as long as you have made at least 9 of your past 12 mortgage payments on time. The goal of the program is to help homeowners who are nearly able to cover the cost of a fixed-rate mortgage. It is not meant to bail out homeowners who took out an option-payment ARM that had an initial rate that was 50% less than what the fully amortizing (regular) cost would have been without the insane teaser rate. At most, the plan is expected to offer refinancing relief to 400,000 homeowners. That sounds like a lot of help—until you realize that Moody's Economy.com forecasts that 3.5 million homes may be lost to foreclosure and short sales in 2009 and 2010.

The big $700 billion bailout bill that passed in October 2008 amended the federal program Hope for Homeowners that was passed in July and put into effect in October. Under this program, homeowners who bought a house before 2008 and have a monthly mortgage payment that exceeds 31% of their gross income may be eligible to refinance into a 30-year, fixed-rate mortgage based on 90% or higher of the home's current value, thereby reducing the monthly mortgage payment. In return for rewriting the mortgage, the FHA agrees to insure the mortgage. The program is currently scheduled to end on September 30, 2011. Three big caveats: Lenders do not have to participate in Hope for Homeowners, and it is not clear if many will, given that the program requires lenders to write down the value of modified mortgages, meaning they have to be willing to take a big loss. Morever, borrowers will face hefty fees and charges. And only mortgages under $550,440 are eligible. The FHA in November 2008 was projecting 13,300 borrowers would be helped in its first year. Go to www.hud.gov and type "Hope for Homeowners" in the search box.

Another initiative scheduled to begin December 15, 2008, is the "Streamlined Modification Program," aimed at mortgages owned or guaranteed by Fannie Mae and Freddie Mac. Homeowners who have missed at least three loan payments, are not in bankruptcy, and can prove a hardship or change in financial circumstances, could qualify for a streamlined workout designed to reduce monthly mortgage payments to 38% of monthly income. To get to that level, the lender can use one or more of these options: extending the term of the loan to 40 years; lowering the interest rate temporarily or permanently; or excluding part of the loan balance when calculating the monthly payment—an option called "principal forbearance." It means the amount you owe won't change, but gets paid back when you sell or refinance the house. Participating servicers will send letters to eligible borrowers; you can also call your servicer to see if you qualify.

WEB SITE ALERT: *Please check www.suzeorman.com for the most up-to-date information on government programs to assist homeowners with unaffordable mortgages. As this book went to press, the FDIC was pushing for a more comprehensive mortgage modification program, but had not yet garnered the backing of the Treasury Department.*

SITUATION: Your mortgage has become too expensive, but you don't want to lose your home and upset your family.

ACTION: If you can't negotiate a lower payment with your lender and none of the programs mentioned above can help you, then I am so sorry to tell you that you must try to sell your home sooner rather than later. I know it is excruciatingly painful to consider, but it is also a simple decision. You cannot stay in a home you cannot afford. Remember, the right moves in 2009 are honest moves.

SITUATION: You're thinking that if you can just hold on to your home for another year, the market will recover and you will be able to refinance your mortgage.

ACTION: Do not base your decisions today on the magical hope that somehow everything will work out if you can just wait for the big rebound.

I have to tell you, it's not coming. At least not in 2009. If you are in an area that has been hard hit, I think it is far more likely you could see another 10%–15% drop in home values in 2009 than a 10%–15% rise.

My best-case scenario for home values in 2009 and probably into 2010 is that efforts to address the credit crisis and the wave of foreclosures begin to take hold and that leads to a gradual stabilization of real estate values. If you think graphically, imagine the capital letter L. Your home's value two years ago was at the top of the L. Since then it has been sliding straight down in value. In 2009–2010, you should be relieved if what we see is that the downstroke stops and we move to the right—that is, prices stop going down. I wish I could tell you that home prices will be more like the letter V: After the big fall, they will quickly bounce back to where they were. But I, too, am committed to being honest. And honestly, there is no chance we will see that. In fact, in the hardest-hit markets it could be years before we see a rebound that brings prices close to their 2006 highs.

If the only way you can hang on depends on a fast and dramatic rebound, your honest move in 2009 is to try and sell your home.

SITUATION: When you bought your home three years ago, the lender steered you into an ARM and said that you would be able to refinance before the first rate adjustment. But now you're being told you can't refinance because you have no equity in the home.

ACTION: Make sure to check in with the lender to see if you can qualify for a loan modification. As I mentioned earlier, there is a growing effort by lenders to help "qualified" borrowers stay in their homes rather than being foreclosed on. But if you are turned down for a loan modification and you will not be able to afford the mortgage when your interest rate resets, then I am so sorry to say it is better to try to sell your home sooner rather than later.

SITUATION: To eke by and make the mortgage payment, you have resorted to using your credit card to cover more expenses. You credit card balance is now ballooning out of control.

ACTION: Again, push to see if your mortgage can be modified. If not, you must consider selling, because using your credit card is not a good solution to this difficult problem. You need to look a few months into the future and realize that sooner rather than later you will have reached your card's credit limit. Then what? You will have a ton of credit card debt and a mortgage you still can't afford. All you have done is delay the inevitable, and in the process you have added thousands of dollars in credit card debt.

For those of you who are stubborn and want to use your credit cards to help you stay in your house, I need you to review what I explained in "Action Plan: Credit." I have never advocated piling on credit card debt, but doing so in 2009 is doubly dangerous. Credit card companies are dealing with their own new reality: They risk massive losses if consumers fall on hard times during the credit crisis and economic recession. They are especially wary of anyone who seems to be heading for trouble; a rising unpaid balance will set off warning bells at the credit card company. It can result in your credit limit being cut, your account being shut down (you won't be able to make new charges, but you will still be responsible for your existing balance), and your interest rate could skyrocket. Please don't compound your mortgage problem with a credit card problem.

I know this is hard to consider, but if you really

can't afford the mortgage today, it is better to move than to go deeper into debt trying to hold on. Of course, I am assuming you have done absolutely everything possible to come up with the money to pay the mortgage. In "Action Plan: Spending," I have suggestions about how to cut your expenses so you have more money left to pay the mortgage or address other financial goals.

SITUATION: You want to make a withdrawal from your 401(k) and use the money to help you keep current with your mortgage payments.

ACTION: Don't do it. If you use up your retirement money today, what will you live on in retirement?

I see so many people making this huge mistake these days. I understand the thinking: You are desperate to hang on to your house and will do anything not to fall into foreclosure. So you empty out your 401(k), paying income tax on the withdrawal and may also be hit with a 10% penalty for money taken out before you are 59½. But then, six months later, you find yourself back in the same hole: You have used up all the money you withdrew from your 401(k) and you are once again falling behind on your mortgage. So all you have done is delay the inevitable: that you can't really afford this mortgage. But in the process you have wiped out any retirement savings. For nothing.

It's also important to know that money you have in a 401(k) or IRA is protected if you ever have to file bankruptcy. You get to keep that money no matter what. This isn't a pleasant scenario to ponder, but let's think about what happens in a really dire situation: You have $20,000 in your 401(k) that you withdraw. After tax and the 10% penalty, you are left with about $15,000. That helps pay the bills for another few months, but once you have used it up, you are back where you started: You can't afford the home. So you lose the home. And now you have no retirement savings.

If instead you kept the $15,000 invested for another 10 years and it earned even a conservative 5% return, you would have nearly $25,000 saved up. And that money will never be taken away in a bankruptcy.

SITUATION: You want to take a loan from your 401(k) and use the money to help you keep current with your mortgage payments.

ACTION: A loan is no better than a withdrawal in this situation. Don't do it. You probably know I am not a big fan of this move. Taking out a loan means you end up being taxed twice on the money you withdraw. And there's the risk that if you are laid off you typically must pay back the loan within a few months. We all know that the current economic weakness makes it likely that we could see even more layoffs in 2009. So if you take out the loan, get laid off, and can't pay it back ASAP, you will run into another tax problem: The loan is treated as a withdrawal and you are stuck paying the 10% early-withdrawal penalty (if you are under 59½) as well as income tax.

SITUATION: You can't afford your mortgage payments, but what you owe on your mortgage is more than the house will sell for.

ACTION: Push your lender to agree to a short sale.

In a short sale, the lender accepts whatever you can sell your house for in today's market, even if that is less than the outstanding balance on your mortgage. The lender is agreeing that once you hand over all proceeds from the sale, your mortgage will be considered settled; any shortfall between the sale price and your balance will be forgiven.

Lenders may be open to this arrangement if they believe what they can get from the short sale is more than the cost they will incur if they foreclose on your home. That said, it is by no means easy to get lenders to agree to a short sale. But it is worth asking. The impact on your FICO credit score is no different from what it would be if you went through foreclosure (see details below), but it is a less traumatic way to walk away.

SITUATION: You are worried a short sale will hurt your FICO score.

ACTION: It will, but it is better to be honest now than hang on and make your financial life (and credit score) even worse by trying to stay in an unaffordable home.

The mortgage you took out was a legal contract in which you agreed to repay the amount you borrowed (the principal) plus interest. In a short sale, you are allowed to repay less than the amount you borrowed. You did not live up to your end of the contract, and that is going to hurt your FICO score. A short sale will stay on your credit report for 7 years (though you won't see the term "short sale" on your credit report; lenders use different terms, sometimes describing short sales as "settled"), the same as a foreclosure. The impact of a short sale (and foreclosure) on your FICO score lessens as time goes by.

If you anticipate you will go through a short sale in 2009, it becomes extra important to keep your credit card balances paid off. I know this is difficult, given the fact that you are dealing with serious financial issues, but you need to make this a priority, because once your FICO score drops because of the short sale, your credit card company may get nervous and that typically leads to raising your interest rate. And the last thing you can afford is a credit card balance with a 32% interest rate.

SITUATION: You have heard that if you agree to a short sale you will have a big tax bill from the IRS, and you don't have the money to pay for that.

ACTION: Relax. You will not owe income tax on the amount of the debt that is forgiven, as long as the short sale occurs before 2012. Originally, the Mortgage Debt Relief Act of 2007 waived the income-tax rule on forgiven debt through 2009, but it was extended to 2012 in the big $700 billion bailout bill of 2008. Up to $2 million in forgiven debt is shielded from income tax for married couples filing a joint tax return ($1 million for individuals).

SITUATION: You were turned down for a short sale. Is foreclosure your only option?

ACTION: Probably. Your only other option is a "deed in lieu of foreclosure," where you hand over the deed to your home to the lender, who then takes the house without going through the formal foreclosure process. While this is an option, it is not widely offered by lenders. Short sale or foreclosure is a more likely alternative if you cannot agree to a loan modification and need to let go of the house.

SITUATION: Will you have to move out immediately when the bank starts the foreclosure process?

ACTION: Foreclosure law varies by state. Lenders will typically start the foreclosure process once you are three months behind in payments.

In about half the states, foreclosures must go through the court system; the other half use procedures that don't require judicial action. For example, some states allow for what is known as a "power of sale," in which mortgage companies—or whoever is empowered under the mortgage document—can handle the foreclosure process. In either type of foreclosure, you will receive notification from the foreclosing party that the foreclosure process has started; typically you will have from a few weeks to a few months (depending on your state's laws) to reinstate the loan by paying up what you owe. (For a roundup of state's foreclosure statutes, see Stephen Elias's *Foreclosure Survival Guide*, Nolo Press, 2008; updates to the list will be published in the legal updates area on nolo.com.)

If you do not get current on your mortgage in the allotted time, the foreclosure proceeds, and your home is sold or the lender takes possession. Though you have the right to remain in your home until you are ordered out by a court after the foreclosure sale, many lenders encourage foreclosed owners to leave by making a "cash for keys" offer, money paid for your leaving voluntarily instead of requiring the new owner to obtain a court eviction order. A good overview of the foreclosure process is at http://www.credit.com/life_stages/overcoming/Understanding-Foreclosure.jsp.

SITUATION: You've been contacted by a foreclosure "rescue specialist" who promises to help you avoid foreclosure for a fee.

ACTION: Don't fall for this. Legitimate foreclosure consultants do not seek you out; you go to them. The huge number of at-risk borrowers has created a whole new opportunity for scam artists who can easily find victims by scouting public records for notices of default. The most common ploy: They'll offer to negotiate a deal with your lender if you pay the fee first; once you pay, they're gone. An even nastier scam involves getting you to sign documents for a new loan that will supposedly make your existing mortgage current, but instead you've been tricked into surrendering title to the scammer in exchange for a "rescue" loan.

If you're facing foreclosure, get help you can trust. Start with the National Foundation for Consumer Credit Counseling, which will put you in touch with a housing counselor in your area: call 866-557-2227. More information on foreclosure scams is available at their Homeowner Crisis Resource Center, housinghelpnow.org, and at the

FTC site, www.ftc.gov/bcp/edu/pubs/consumer/credit/cre42.shtm. If you think you've been a victim of foreclosure fraud, contact the Federal Trade Commission at ftc.gov or call 1-877-FTC-HELP, or your state attorney general's office.

SITUATION: You are worried that going through a foreclosure means you will never be able to buy another house.

ACTION: You will be eligible to buy a house in the future if you take steps today to start rebuilding your FICO score. There is no sugarcoating this: A foreclosure, as well as a short sale, will be a big negative mark on your FICO credit score. But it is not a permanent stain. The foreclosure stays on your credit report for seven years; each year its impact on your FICO credit score lessens. This is no different from a short sale.

Because you will likely see your FICO score drop, you want to do your best to reduce any unpaid credit card balances if you anticipate going through foreclosure in 2009. I know this is going to be hard to pull off, given that you are obviously dealing with some serious financial challenges. But please do your best to keep your credit card balance low. When your FICO score goes down in 2009, your credit card company may become nervous that you are in trouble. That might result in the card company's lowering your credit line. And as we discussed in "Action Plan: Credit," that starts a vicious cycle that can lead to a huge increase in your interest rate.

SITUATION: With real estate prices falling, you are wondering if it's a good time to buy a home.

ACTION: I still believe that over time a home can be one of the most satisfying investments you can make, but you have to make sure you can afford it. By "afford it" I mean not just being about to meet the monthly mortgage payments and expenses, but you have to be able to make those payments for at least eight months if you don't have income coming in. Why eight months? Because if by chance you were to lose your job, it could take many months to find a new one. I certainly hope you would find a great new job quickly, but if we find ourselves in a deep, slow recession, it could take longer to find a job than you anticipate. I want you to be in a position to know you have savings set aside to cover the mortgage while you job-hunt.

As for timing: I recommend buying in 2009 only if you intend to stay put for at least five years. I don't care what sort of deal you think you can get, it makes no sense to buy a home today if you suspect you might move in a few years. This housing recovery is going to be slow (remember the L scenario I mentioned earlier). If you buy today, prices may not go up much over the next few years;

in fact, in some areas they could still go down. And it's important to remember that when you go to sell you will be responsible for paying an agent a sales commission of 5%–6%. That could wipe out any appreciation you might see over the next year or two . . . or three, depending on how hard hit your area is.

And don't even think about buying if you have yet to save up at least 10% of the purchase price for a down payment. Did I say 10%? I should add that 20% is even better. Though there are some government programs that require smaller down payments, the new reality is that the only way many homeowners will qualify for a regular mortgage is if they can make a solid down payment.

The last requirement I have for potential buyers is that you can buy your home with a standard 30-year, fixed-rate mortgage. Instead of "betting" on an adjustable-rate loan, or that you will have enough equity in three or five years to refinance, I think it is smarter to stick with a 30-year fixed-rate so you never have to worry about your payment rising.

SILVER LINING: *The Housing and Economic Recovery Act (July 2008) gives a credit of up to $7,500 for first-time buyers who purchase a home between April 9, 2008, and July 1, 2009. Individuals with income below $75,000 and married couples with income below $150,000 are eligible for this program. The credit is actually an interest-free loan. You claim* *it on your federal tax return and then repay the amount of your credit over a 15-year period.*

SITUATION: You want to take advantage of the low real estate prices in your area, but there's no way you can afford a 10% down payment.

ACTION: If you can't afford a 10% down payment, then you probably can't afford to buy in 2009.

Though there are some federal loan programs that require down payments of less than 5%, if you want a conventional mortgage, lenders this year are going to insist on down payments of 10%, and in many instances you will need to have 20% to be offered the best interest rates.

The days of no-down-payment loans are gone, and with any luck they will never return. You have to realize that if the millions of homeowners who bought a house with no down payment during the housing boom had been required to make a down payment, we would not be in this mess right now. Without the down payment, those people would not have been allowed to buy in the first place.

And I have always said that if you can't afford to make a down payment, it's a sign you can't afford a home.

SITUATION: You don't know what purchase price you can afford for a house.

ACTION: First-time buyers must understand that paying $1,000 in monthly rent does not mean you can afford a mortgage of $1,000 a month. In addition to the base mortgage, you will also have to pay property tax, home insurance, and, if your down payment is less than 20%, private mortgage insurance. You also have to be ready to pay for repairs and maintenance costs—you're the landlord now! If you add up all those other non-mortgage costs, your monthly bill can be 30% to 40% more than the basic mortgage. So if you were to take on a $1,000 mortgage, your monthly housing costs could actually be closer to $1,300–$1,400 a month. Yes, it is true that you will get a tax break as a homeowner; the interest on your mortgage payments is tax-deductible. That's a help, but not a solution.

The best way to figure out how much you can afford is to use an online calculator (go to www.bankrate.com) to figure out the base mortgage amount. Then add at least 30% to that amount and ask yourself if you can honestly handle that cost. If not, look to buy a less expensive home. The goal is to afford a home comfortably, not to stretch and gamble.

SITUATION: You bought your house 10 years ago and have a lot of equity, but you wonder if you should sell now and just rent.

ACTION: Your home is not a stock that you buy and sell based on its short-term value. If you enjoy your home, if you can afford your home, and if you don't need to sell right now, stay put.

I have to tell you, the time to sell was about three years ago during the market peak. It's no different from my advice for how to look at investing. If you have time on your side, be patient. If you will need cash from the sale within the next year or two, then that's a different matter. We could indeed see prices fall farther from current levels before the housing market stabilizes. Assuming you don't have to move, why move? Especially when you consider that you'll have to pay the 6% sales commission along with the cost and hassle of the actual move.

SITUATION: Your son and daughter-in-law are in mortgage trouble. You are retired and are considering using some of your savings to help them through this rough patch.

ACTION: If you can afford to help, then of course help. But that's a serious issue you need to carefully ponder. If helping them out today in any way puts your own retirement security at risk, then you simply cannot afford to help. That's not being selfish, it's actually looking out for your kids. You need to think through how this could play out.

You help the kids out now, but that means your retirement account runs dry in 15 years instead of lasting the 25 or 30 years you were counting on. And let's say you have the good fortune of living a very long life. Only problem is, you need to turn to your kids for help because you no longer have any money left.

You have the valuable assets in this situation. You probably own your own home outright and you have a nice retirement fund. Do not put those at risk. If your kids are in a house they can't afford, it may be best for them to let go. If they live nearby, you can offer to have them move in while they regroup. Or if they are determined to stay in the house, how about you offer to take a more active role helping with the grandkids on the weekends so they can take on part-time work—or extra projects at their job—to bring in the income they need.

SITUATION: Two years ago, you took out a HELOC that you never used but kept in case you ran into an emergency. Your lender just told you it was revoking your HELOC.

ACTION: You must have a regular savings account funded with your own cash in 2009; you cannot rely on either a HELOC or credit card line of credit to be available in an emergency. Home equity lines of credit are being rescinded (or reduced) because of falling home values. With less equity in your home, you suddenly look a lot riskier to your HELOC lender.

SITUATION: You have an open HELOC and are wondering if you should tap it now and put the money into a savings account to serve as your emergency savings fund.

ACTION: Fund a savings account from real savings, not by increasing your debt. It is absurd to take on more debt in 2009, given the likelihood that in a recession you have an increased risk of losing your job. Don't tell me you will just use your savings to cover the HELOC payment if you get laid off. Wake up. You will need that money to pay your basic living costs, so why would you want to add to that monthly nut?

If you want to build a real, honest savings account, check out my advice in "Action Plan: Spending," for ways to find money to put toward your most important goals in 2009.

SITUATION: You planned on using a HELOC to help pay for your child's college costs, but with home values down so much you doubt you will be able to pay for school with a HELOC.

ACTION: Be grateful market forces didn't lure you into this bad move. I have never liked it when families increase their housing debt to pay for school. It typically leaves parents severely in debt just at the point when they should be focusing on paying off their mortgage debt, not increasing it, to prepare for retirement.

Don't worry, you have solid loan options to cover college costs. Please check out "Action Plan: Paying for College."

SITUATION: You were counting on booming home prices to help pay for your retirement.

ACTION: Time to get serious about saving money from your paycheck. As I stated earlier in this chapter, I am still a big believer that your home is a solid long-term investment. But that means it will, on average, rise in value at a pace that is only one percentage point or so ahead of inflation. That's not going to fill your retirement nest egg.

If you are over 50, make it your goal to take advantage of the extra "catch-up" amounts you are allowed to invest in your 401(k) and IRA. In 2009, you can invest an extra $5,500 in your 401(k) if you are over 50, for a total maximum contribution of $22,000. You can also contribute an extra $1,000 to your IRA in 2009, for a total of $6,000.

Can't imagine where to come up with extra cash? Make sure you read "Action Plan: Spending."

SITUATION: You can afford your home, but you worry that you have made a lousy investment.

ACTION: Love your home for what it is. Yes, it is an investment, but not one whose value you should be charting on a monthly or annual basis. If you can afford your home today, the best thing you can do is not worry about the current turmoil in the housing market.

Homes remain a solid long-term investment. But let's review what I mean by solid. The long-term trend—and I am talking decades, not a few years—is that homes on average rise in value at a pace that is about one percentage point better than inflation. I think that when the real estate market stabilizes—and yes, it is a matter of when, not if—it is certainly reasonable to expect that housing will return to a more typical (lower) appreciation rate. One way to look at the massive bursting of the real estate bubble is that it is in fact a painful correction that brings things back to a level based on a more moderate rate of appreciation.

In the meantime, your home is where you live. It is a refuge, a place where you and your family build memories. It is also a fine tax break.

SITUATION: You are near retirement age and planned on paying off your mortgage ahead of schedule. You're not sure that still makes sense.

ACTION: If you are in a home you plan to live in forever, I think 2009 is a fabulous time to accelerate your mortgage payments. The only caveat: If you have credit card debt to pay off, make that your priority in 2009. And always make sure you invest enough in your 401(k) to receive the company match.

If you have all that taken are of, then paying down your mortgage makes plenty of sense. I have always been a proponent of getting rid of mortgage debt before you retire. The best way to ensure that you will be able to afford your home in retirement is to know you own it free and clear and have to use retirement funds only for property tax and maintenance costs.

If you own your home free and clear, you also have the option of borrowing money through a reverse mortgage if you find you need extra income in retirement.

SITUATION: You rent a home and have always paid your landlord on time, but you just found out you have to move out because the landlord did not pay the mortgage and the bank is foreclosing on the home.

ACTION: You need to push very hard for your rights. While there was increased awareness as 2008 progressed that renters were innocent victims of the foreclosure crisis, the solutions to date are not ironclad laws that ensure every renter is safe. The $700 billion bailout bill included a provision that "where permissible" will allow renters who are current on their rent to remain in a property that is taken over by one of the federal bailout plans. But that's only if the loan becomes part of the federal bailout and it doesn't run afoul of existing state laws. There is also some vague language in the same bill that says the Treasury Department can lean on lenders seeking federal assistance to not evict renters who are on time with their payments.

I encourage you to be very aggressive and relentless in pushing to stay in your home. The National Low Income Housing Coalition has an online chart of what protections exist for tenants in the various states; its evolving research is available at http://www.nlihc.org/doc/State-Foreclosure-Chart.pdf. I wish there were somewhere I could send you for the best local resources, but alas, none exists. So you need to start calling and e-mailing like crazy to find out what is going on in your state and county. Start with a local government or nonprofit tenant advocacy organization. If you have a local legal aid office or a housing assistance program, check in with them. The bottom line, unfortunately, is that you need to be your own most vocal advocate. But in the down market of 2009, there may be some opportunity to convince a lender to honor a lease, so the rental unit remains occupied.

SITUATION: You are in good shape financially, with enough money to put down 20%. You wonder if 2009 is the right time to get a good deal on a vacation home so you can rent it out and make some money.

ACTION: Be very careful here. Many of you looking to buy vacation homes or investment real estate may not be looking at the big picture, and that could get you in trouble. If you need to rent out this property in order to make the mortgage payments, then I would say do not touch this "opportunity" with a 10-foot pole. Why? Because if something happens and your tenants cannot pay the rent, how are you going to pay the mortgage? You need to know that you can afford the payments month in and month out, regardless of rental income. Remember, too, that in times like these more vacation-home owners are apt to want to rent out their properties, and that's bad for you. More competition, that is, for fewer potential renters.

And at the risk of repeating myself, let me say yet again: If you have one penny of credit card debt, if you do not have retirement savings, if you do not have an emergency savings fund that can cover your living costs for at least eight months, if you are still paying off your primary mortgage or have an outstanding HELOC balance, you cannot afford a vacation home. In 2009 or any year. Denied!

8

ACTION PLAN

Paying for College

The New Reality

Gone are the days when all you had to do to save money for your kids' education was to put money every single month into a 529 plan, sit back, and watch it grow. Also gone are the days when you could consider taking out a home equity line of credit or taking a loan from your 401(k) to cover college costs when a little extra help was needed.

So what exactly happened that makes all these options obsolete? Simple: Real estate and stock values have decreased dramatically in a very short period of time, leaving many of you high and dry when it comes to paying for college. But that's not all. While the real estate and stock markets were in turmoil, the United States economy was also experiencing a credit crisis.

While this crisis had and is still having a devastating effect on the world's economy, resulting in a series of Treasury bailouts capped by the $700 billion rescue plan, it is also having a tremendous effect on you, the individual. Suddenly, money you were going to use to pay for college just isn't there, and the credit crunch has you worried you won't be able to take out college loans to make up for your shortfall. But I am here to tell you that sometimes even an economic crisis of this magnitude comes with a silver lining.

The good news that came out of this credit crunch is that Congress passed emergency legislation in May 2008 that got the student loan market flowing again. This new legislation includes significant changes that increase the amounts students can borrow from the federal government and ease the terms of repaying these loans. So out of all the bad economic news comes this piece of great news: In 2009, most families will be able to bypass expensive and risky private loans altogether and pay for college using loans from the federal government.

However, how to proceed is not quite so simple. Your plan of action depends on a variety of factors, including your age and the age of your children and how much, if any, money you have to put toward a college education. As you read on below and devise your own 2009 college fund Action Plan, I ask that you be ruthlessly honest about what you can and cannot afford.

What you must do in 2009

- If your child is heading to college within four years and your college savings are in the stock market, you should begin to phase it out of the market, so that you are 100% out by the time he or she is 17.
- If you have a child who will enter college in 2009–2010, look into getting a Stafford loan.
- If Stafford loans are not enough, parents should consider a PLUS loan. Significant changes to this program last year make this a viable option for many more families.
- Stay away from private student loans at all costs.
- If you are graduating from college in 2009 with student loan debt, know your repayment options.

Your 2009 Action Plan: Paying for College

SITUATION: Your child is set to go to college next year. Given the shaky state of the stock market, you want to stop putting money in your 401(k) and use those funds to pay for your child's education. Should you?

ACTION: No, no, no. Your retirement account must come first.

This year, there is nothing—and I mean nothing—that takes precedence over locking in short-term security (in the form of an eight-month emergency savings account) and providing for long-term security by continuing to invest for your retirement.

I am not insensitive to the importance you place on providing the opportunity for your children to achieve and realize their greatest potential in life. And I am aware that it is not an easy thing to do to ask that your children share the cost of college by taking out student loans. But it is necessary—especially now. It could be years before the stock market fully recovers. Your 401(k) has taken a beating, but as counterintuitive as it may seem, I am asking you to keep buying shares of the investments that you have in your 401(k) plan. I am assuming that your money is invested in good-quality funds and that you are diversified. I'm also assuming that you have 10 years or longer until retirement. Here's why it makes sense to keep contributing to your plan: The more the market goes down, the more shares you will be able to buy of the mutual funds you are invested in, and the more money you will make when the stock market comes back.

Most important to keep in mind is that you need that money waiting for you in retirement. If it's not there, you could end up being a financial burden for your kids. If you fail to save today, what will you have to live on in retirement? Now, don't worry, I am not suggesting you leave your kids high and dry. As I explain in the following pages, both your child and you can take out federal loans to help pay for school.

SITUATION: Your college savings fund took such a hit, you want to borrow from your 401(k) to cover the college bills.

ACTION: Don't you dare. It is never smart to touch your retirement savings to pay for another expense. And in 2009 it is doubly risky, given the possibility of increasing layoffs; if that happens, any outstanding loan must be repaid within a few months or the loan is considered a withdrawal. That will trigger income tax on the entire amount you withdrew and typically a 10% early-withdrawal penalty if you are under 59½ years old. If you need to come up with money for college, federal loans are the best option.

SITUATION: You want to use IRA savings to pay for your child's college tuition.

ACTION: As I said earlier, raiding your retirement funds to pay for college is not ideal. What will you live on in retirement? Another potential problem is that taking an early distribution from an IRA can affect your child's financial aid eligibility; the withdrawal will be treated as parental income, and that is a major factor in determining aid. My advice: Don't touch your IRA to pay for college.

For those of you who refuse to follow this advice, I do want to point out that if you withdraw money early from your IRA to pay for college costs you will not owe the 10% early withdrawal penalty typically charged by the IRS on withdrawals made before age 59½. You may, however, owe income tax on the withdrawn money. Withdrawals of money you contributed to a Roth IRA will not be taxed, though earnings may be taxed. Money withdrawn from a traditional IRA may be subject to income tax.

SITUATION: You told your child you would send her to a private college, but you lost your job and now you can't afford it.

ACTION: Times have changed and so must you. You have to be more realistic and honest with your kids than ever before. I want all parents to seriously rethink what they can afford to spend on college, be it through loans or out-of-pocket savings. The best school for your child is one that provides a solid education and doesn't put the family $150,000 to $200,000 in debt. I have no patience for anyone who tells me "cost is not the issue—a quality education is more important." *People, cost is a huge issue.* You can't afford to take on debt that keeps you from being able to pay your bills or to save for your retirement. Nor does it make sense to let your child pile up $100,000 in private student loans. Student loan debt, in most cases, is not forgiven in bankruptcy. It is the Velcro of debt; you cannot shake loose from it. Student loan debt will make it that much harder for your children to build their own financial security after they graduate. When you have a lot of student loan debt, it makes it harder to qualify for a mortgage or a car loan. And I cannot tell you how many smart, well-intentioned young adults tell me they had no idea how much their monthly payments would be and they cannot afford to pay them at all.

Keep an open mind: Look for affordable schools, starting, of course, with your in-state college system. A quality education is not dependent on price. You can find a great fit for your child and your finances if you make it a priority. Go to Kiplinger.com and under "Your Money" click on "Best College Values."

SITUATION: You have no credit card debt and your retirement savings is on track, so you want to start a college savings fund, but you are not sure about the best way to invest.

ACTION: A 529 Savings Plan is one of the easiest and smartest ways to save for future college costs. Money you invest in a plan grows tax-deferred, and eventual withdrawals will be tax-free if they are used for "qualified" college costs. There is also no income-eligibility requirement; all families can set up a 529, and contributions can come from parents, grandparents, aunts, uncles, friends. In addition to 529 plans, there are indeed other savings options, such as Coverdell Educational Savings Accounts and U.S. savings bonds. I highly recommend you check out the Web site www.savingforcollege.com; it is hands-down the most informative site for parents who want to save for their kids' future college costs.

SITUATION: You have been putting money into a 529 plan every month since your little one was born. The stock market scares you these days, so you're thinking you should move your money out of your plan's stock fund choice and into bonds or cash offered by the 529 plan. Good idea?

ACTION: Nooo. If you have at least 10 years until you need your money, you have time on your side to ride out volatility in the stock market. You don't want to stop investing in stocks, or pull out of stocks when you have time on your side; the smart move is to invest *more* in your 529 plan's stock fund in 2009. Your money will buy more shares of that fund when prices are low (as they are now). The more shares you accumulate now, the more money you will make when stocks rebound. If your child is five years old, you have time on your side to wait for that rebound.

SITUATION: Big losses in your 529 have you so worried you want to quit the 529 and move all the money into a safe bank account.

ACTION: Do not do this, because it can have significant tax consequences. Money you leave in a 529 that is eventually used to pay for college expenses is free of federal tax and state income tax too (except in Alabama, should you use a non-Alabama 529). But if you pull the money out, you can be hit with a 10% penalty tax on any earnings on that account. Below you will find my recommendations for the right mix of stocks and bonds in your 529, based on your child's age. If you feel you simply can't stand to remain invested in stocks, then shift the money into a stable-value account within the 529.

That said, I recognize some of you may still feel compelled to close the account and withdraw the money. If you've had a hefty loss, there may be a way for you to deduct nearly all of that from your taxable income, but you will want a trusted tax advisor guiding you on this. The tax break involves deducting your 529 losses as a miscellaneous itemized deduction on your income tax return—but you can deduct those only to the extent that they exceed 2 percent of your adjusted gross income.

Because of the complexity involved in doing this—especially if your state allowed partial or full income tax deductions on your contributions, and the workings of the alternative minimum tax—I can't emphasize enough how important it is to get good advice if you choose to go this route.

SITUATION: Your child starts college in two years and your 529 is 100% in stocks, so it has taken a big hit. You don't know if you should move out of stocks now to avoid further losses.

ACTION: You should have started moving out of stocks a few years ago. When your child is within a year or two of freshman year, you no longer have time on your side. You are going to have to start using that money sooner rather than later, so you need to make sure your money is safe and sound in the 529 plan's bond or money market fund. My recommendation is that you slowly shift money out of stocks and into bonds starting at age 14. You goal should be that you are completely out of stocks by the time your child is five years from *senior year in college*—typically, that is age 17.

Under age 14:	100% stocks
Age 14:	75% stocks
Age 15:	50% stocks
Age 16:	25% stocks
Age 17:	0% stocks

If your current allocation exceeds those targets, I recommend you rebalance your portfolio ASAP. I wish I could tell you to wait for a nice big rebound in your portfolio, but you do not have time on your side. There is no guarantee that the rebound will come between now and when you have to begin writing the checks for college.

Those of you who have opted for a fund in your 529 plan that automatically changes its allocation as your child gets closer to college still need to pay attention and understand how much you will have invested in stocks when your child hits 14, 15, 16, 17, and 18. I have seen plans with up to 50% in stocks a year or two before the child will enter school. That's unacceptable at any time, and it is especially risky in 2009, when we have to anticipate more market volatility.

If you find your target fund overloads on stocks close to college, I recommend moving out of the target option, finding the best low-cost stock and bond fund options offered by the plan, and putting your money in both those funds according to the strategy above.

SITUATION: You have time on your side, but after watching your child's college fund plummet, you just can't stomach keeping the entire portfolio invested in stocks.

ACTION: It's fine to move up to 20% into bonds. A small amount of bonds will reduce your portfolio's overall loss in a bear market, and if that helps you stay committed to investing and helps you sleep better, then it is the right move for you.

SITUATION: You tried to move money out of your 529 plan's stock fund and into the bond fund option, but you were told you had to wait until next year.

ACTION: Understand that an IRS rule requires 529 plans to limit participants to rebalancing their portfolio just once a year. The reasoning is that you can't be trusted to be a patient long-term investor, so this rule was meant to keep you from day-trading your kid's college fund. As if.

So if you have already rebalanced your portfolio for 2009, you may have to wait until 2010 to make your switch out of stocks. Because of this rule, it is imperative to get your asset allocation right so you don't need to make any midyear corrections. As I explain above, once your child is 14 you need to start dialing down how much of your college fund is invested in stocks.

SITUATION: Your family doesn't qualify for financial aid (or the aid package isn't as much as you expected), but you don't have money to pay the college bills this year.

ACTION: First, you need to take a deep breath. I know it is stressful. I know it is upsetting. But you do have options. One of the great misconceptions is that federal loans are only for students and families that meet certain income-eligibility rules. That is absolutely incorrect. In addition to the many forms of aid and loans that are income-based, there are also affordable loans available for students and parents regardless of family wealth or income. If you find that your school's financial aid package for 2009–2010 is not enough to cover all your costs, you can supplement that aid with non-income-based loans.

The first step is for your child, the student, to apply for both subsidized and unsubsidized Stafford loans. Yes, your child borrows first, not you. Staffords are the cheapest loan options. If you want to make a side agreement with your child that you will help with the repayment of the Staffords, that's fine. But please get over any concern or guilt about having your child borrow first.

If you meet income-eligibility rules, your child may qualify for a subsidized Stafford loan. (It is typically part of a financial aid package you receive from the school.) Subsidized means the federal government pays the interest on the loan while your kid is in school. The interest rate for a subsidized loan is 6% for the 2008–2009 school year and 5.6% for the 2009–2010 school year. But here's what so many people fail to understand:

Anyone, regardless of income, can apply for an unsubsidized Stafford. The interest rate is fixed at 6.8% and interest payments are the responsibility of the student. The student can opt to not pay interest while in school and have it added to the loan balance. Here's a suggestion: If Grandma and Grandpa want to know how they can help with school, ask them to cover the Stafford interest payments so their grandchild can graduate with a lower loan balance. If that's not an option, your child can work during school and make the interest payments him- or herself.

SITUATION: How much can you borrow on a Stafford loan in 2009?

ACTION: Thanks to the emergency federal legislation mentioned earlier, the amount you can borrow on a Stafford (combined subsidized and unsubsidized) has been increased by $2,000 a year beginning in the 2008–2009 academic year. Freshmen can now borrow $5,500; sophomores $6,500; and juniors and seniors $7,500. Children who are not claimed as dependents by their parents are eligible for higher amounts.

SITUATION: Your child qualifies for a subsidized loan, but you need more money.

ACTION: Make sure your child applies for an unsubsidized Stafford, too. After maxing out on the subsidized loan, your child is eligible for up to another $2,000 a year in an unsubsidized Stafford. Your school's financial aid office should automatically alert you to this, but the sad fact is that many families leave Stafford money on the table every year because they don't understand the rules about unsubsidized loans.

SITUATION: **What do you have to do to apply for Stafford loans?**

ACTION: There is one big requirement for Stafford loans (and school financial aid): You must complete the Free Application for Federal Student Aid (FAFSA). No FAFSA, no Staffords. It is not a fun form to fill out, but spending a few hours wading through all the financial disclosure is worth it, trust me. Check with the school's financial aid office; they are set up to help you navigate this process.

SITUATION: **You have applied for subsidized and unsubsidized Stafford loans, but you need even more money.**

ACTION: Apply for a Parental PLUS loan, another federal loan program. The parent, not the student, is the borrower. There is no income limit, and you can borrow up to the full amount of college costs minus any aid and other loans. The interest rate is a fixed 8.5% for most borrowers. (It is 7.9% if the school is part of a program that has you borrow directly from the federal government, rather than using a third-party lender. Only 20% or so of schools are part of the Federal Direct Loan program.) But I want to be clear: You apply for a PLUS only after your child has maxed out on the Staffords. A PLUS is a very good deal, but Staffords are even better given their lower interest rates. Staffords first. PLUS second.

SITUATION: **You applied for a PLUS loan in 2007, but you were turned down. Should you apply again?**

ACTION: Yes! If you investigated a PLUS loan a few years ago and didn't like the terms—or if you were turned down—I encourage you to take a fresh look for 2009. The emergency legislation in May 2008 brought about some very big changes designed to make PLUS loans a more viable and affordable option.

Through December 31, 2009, parents will be eligible for a PLUS loan as long as they are no more than 180 days delinquent on a mortgage payment on their primary residence or medical bill payments. Previously, the limit was 90 days or more late on any debt.

There is no FICO credit check per se to obtain a PLUS loan, but your credit history is reviewed to check for any "adverse" actions on your credit profile. Families that have declared bankruptcy in the past five years are not eligible for a PLUS loan. In the past, you also needed to be "current" on your other debt payments (not including mortgage and medical bills), but recognizing the stress families are under to juggle expenses in this rough economy, the emergency legislation gives PLUS lenders more leeway in forgiving debt-payment slipups. Another reason I prefer PLUS loans over private loans is that in the event the parent dies or is permanently disabled, the debt is forgiven; private lenders are not required to forgive debt.

SITUATION: You want to take out a PLUS loan, but you know you can't afford to pay it back immediately.

ACTION: Don't worry—you don't have to. Another helpful piece of the 2008 legislation is that parents no longer have to start repaying a PLUS loan within 60 days of receiving the money. You can now defer repayment until your child graduates. That means you won't have to make loan payments during the four years when you are most likely using some of your monthly income to pay for school costs. The delay also means that families can make repayment of the PLUS a family affair: Legally, the parent is responsible for repayment of the loan, but having your child help with repayment will ease the burden.

SITUATION: You want to help with a PLUS loan, but you are worried about handling the payments over the long term.

ACTION: Before you agree to take out a PLUS loan, you must have a serious talk with your child about how much you expect them to contribute to the eventual repayment of the PLUS. That is an important and honest conversation to have ahead of school. It may spur your child to push extra hard to earn the most money possible during the summer (or work part time during school) to build up some reserves. It might also put the cost for spring break in Cabo—definitely a "want," not a "need"—into perspective.

SITUATION: Your child wants you to cosign a private student loan.

ACTION: Forget private loans and use a PLUS if you plan to help your kid pay for school.

As a result of the credit crisis, student loan lenders have become a lot tighter with their money. This is the same issue we discussed in "Action Plan: Credit." Lenders are now focused on reducing their risk. So while it used to be easy for students to take on tens of thousands of dollars in private student loan debt with little (or no) credit check by lenders, that no longer works. In 2009 (and for the foreseeable future), students who want a private student loan need to have a FICO score of at least 680. Few teenagers have a FICO score. So lenders are now insisting that the student get a cosigner on the loan, and that person needs to have a strong FICO score.

Rather than cosign a private loan, you are far better off applying for a Parental PLUS loan and making it clear to your child that she is expected to repay some or all of the loan once she graduates. Part of my reason for relying on the PLUS program is a simple practical matter: Private loans will not be easily available in 2009 if lenders continue to have a hard time raising money in the troubled credit markets. But even if the storm passes, the private loan skies part, and lenders start plying your kids with offers for easy private loans, I want you to say no. PLUS loans are usually a better choice over private loans. Private student loans have variable rates, and those rates can be 1% to 10% more than a benchmark index. Even if you initially qualify for a competitive interest rate (you'll need a FICO score above 720 to even have a shot), you run the risk of future rate hikes. I'll take the 8.5% fixed rate on the PLUS loan, thank you very much.

SITUATION: You just lost your job and you are in no position to help your kids with their college tuition. What do you do?

ACTION: Contact the financial aid office at each school immediately and let them know about the layoff. There may be more money—aid or loans—based on your changed financial status. But I want to be clear: No school is a bottomless pit, and the sad fact is that many schools—especially public universities—are feeling the economic pinch too. But chances are you may get some extra help from the school. And just to reiterate: Please make sure your child has maxed out on all available Stafford loans. At a maximum fixed rate of 6.8%, it is an affordable way to borrow for school.

You can also obtain a PLUS loan, assuming you are current on your bills, and you can defer payment until your child graduates. By then you should be back at work and your child can also contribute to the PLUS repayment. But I want to be very clear here: You must limit what you borrow to what you can truly afford. I encourage you to go to the College Board's Web site and use its online calculator to see what PLUS loans you take out today will cost to repay: http://apps.collegeboard.com/fincalc/parpay.jsp It is crucial that you go through this exercise with your newfound commitment to honesty front and center. If you will not be able to handle the repayment, do not take out the loan.

If not taking on debt is honestly what is best for you, you must not beat yourself up that you cannot continue to pay for school. I wish I could tell you to "do whatever is necessary" to keep your kid in school right now. But I don't traffic in wishful thinking; I am focused on the realistic actions you must take to ensure your long-term financial security. So here's the bottom line during this very tough economic time: You may need to tell your kids you can't keep paying for school now that your personal economic situation has changed. If that means your child needs to transfer to a less expensive school or take a year off to earn money to cover the costs himself, that is what needs to happen.

I understand how difficult that is to consider, but hard times require making hard choices. Taking on debt you can't afford is never smart; in today's world, with the economic outlook so bleak, you must not take on more than you can realistically handle.

SITUATION: You're about to graduate and you doubt you'll get a job that will pay enough to cover your student loan payments.

ACTION: If you have federal loans, there are a variety of programs you may qualify for that can make repayment more affordable. And beginning in July 2009, there is also a new repayment plan for federal student loans (though not PLUS loans): The Income-Based Repayment Plan will make repayment affordable for graduates who pursue careers in traditionally lower-paying fields such as teaching and public service. The best move you can make is to show up for the exit interview with your financial aid office and learn about your options.

The worst thing any recent graduate can do is assume they can "hide" or "ignore" their student loan debt until they get settled into a job and have the cash flow to handle payments. Big, big mistake. Fall behind on your student loans and you will ruin your credit profile. You need to understand that student loans are debt, and if you don't pay your debts it gets reported to the credit bureaus. Faster than you can say, "Wow, I am so screwed," you have a FICO score below 700. In my book, it's never okay to have a low FICO score, but in 2009 it is flat-out dumb. Yes, dumb. In the past, even if you had a lousy FICO score you could still get what you wanted. The only hassle is that you would have to pay more for everything—a higher deposit for the cell phone, for example, or a higher rate for a car loan. But in 2009, a lousy

FICO score means big trouble. Lenders, landlords, and even employers simply won't want to do business with you. In a world where everyone is trying to reduce their risk, a lousy FICO score brands you as a high risk.

And just to drive home this point: Even if you declare bankruptcy, your student loan debt in most cases will not be forgiven. This is debt you can't outrun.

SITUATION: The job market is terrible and you can't find a job, even with your brand-new degree. You have no clue how you will be able to start repaying your student loans.

ACTION: With federal loans, you can apply for an unemployment deferment; if you are working less than 30 hours a week, you will not have to start repayment. But again, you must *apply* for this deferment. If you simply don't pay, it is going to start showing up on your credit reports as a delinquency. If you have a subsidized federal loan, interest will not continue to build up during this deferment. If your loan is unsubsidized, interest does accrue. Your financial aid office can walk you through all your federal loan repayment options. You can also can get help at the finaid.org Web site.

SITUATION: You graduated with debt from various student loans and you wonder if you should consolidate or not.

ACTION: Consolidating your federal loans is smart. The main advantage is that you can pile together all your loans from the four years of school into one mega-loan that requires just one monthly payment. This will likely keep your FICO score in good shape, because you will find it easier to stay on top of things with a single payment.

The fixed consolidation rate for all Stafford loans issued after July 1, 2006, is 6.8%.

SITUATION: You graduated with private student loans. Can you consolidate them and defer payments?

ACTION: With private student loans you have limited options. You are basically at the mercy of your lender's repayment policy, and they are not required to grant any deferments. It's completely at their discretion. Moreover, the credit crisis has all but shut down the private-loan consolidation market. Right now, that market is all but closed for private borrowers.

SILVER LINING: *The $700 billion bailout bill Congress passed in October 2008 restored a college* *tax break that had expired. Through 2009, you can deduct up to $4,000 in college tuition and fees if your income is below $65,000 for single filers (you can receive a $2,000 deduction if your income is between $65,000 and $80,000) and $130,000 for those married and filing jointly (you get the $2,000 deduction at incomes between $130,000 and $160,000). You can claim this deduction even if you do not file an itemized return.*

9

ACTION PLAN

Protecting Your Family and Yourself

The New Reality

Your job is at risk. This has nothing to do with how talented and well-respected you are, or the fact that your past three reviews have been gold star. You are at risk for reasons that have nothing to do with you. The double whammy of the credit crisis and an economic recession increases the likelihood that businesses will be forced to cut back on costs, and that could mean reducing staff. In this environment, just hoping you will be spared is not the right action. You must take active steps today to make sure your family is safe no matter what happens jobwise in 2009. That means making sure you have savings to pay the bills instead of running up credit card debt or raiding your retirement accounts. It also means having health insurance no matter what and a game plan for landing your next job.

It's important to understand that even if the credit crisis hadn't occurred, 2009 was shaping up to be a tough year for the economy. Our economy is cyclical in nature—there are periods of strong growth and periods of slower growth. Slowdowns are always part of the equation. There is no avoiding them altogether; rather, the goal is that when they do hit, it is with a soft punch rather than a knockout. In an economist's perfect world, what we experience is an orderly winding down from a period of faster growth to slower growth that soon transitions into a new period of even stronger growth. But sometimes real life is less than ideal. If instead the economy slows down with a thud—known, in fact, as a hard landing—we can find ourselves in a recession: a period where the economy doesn't just shift to slower growth, it actually contracts. When that happens, job losses can be very high as companies cut positions to reduce costs.

The continuing problems caused by the credit crisis appear to have ruined our chances of a soft landing in 2009. Unless banks start lending again, companies that were already girding for a slowdown in business are going to be in even bigger trouble. Every business, from the 10-person small company to General Electric, relies on credit.

Short-term credit helps businesses pay the bills and keeps supplies flowing while waiting for clients to pay their bills, as well as enabling firms to finance longer-term expansion projects. Long-term credit is another vital way businesses borrow to grow. If you want to build a new plant or expand your business line, you need money to pay for your expansion before you can expect to earn any money from that new business. When businesses can't borrow money it greatly reduces their ability to expand. Without short-term or long-term credit, a business is going to find it doubly tough to get through the economic slowdown. I am not saying we are guaranteed to have a deep and hard landing in 2009. But it is definitely a possibility if businesses can't get credit. And let's face it: 2009 is not going to be a great year for consumer spending; that's driven much of our economic growth in past years, but you and I both know that you are focusing on spending less and saving more in 2009.

What I do know for sure is that in times like these, my saying "hope for the best, prepare for the worst" could not be more apt. You can't keep the bad times from happening, but you can keep them from decimating your financial security. There are actions you need to take now to make sure that no matter what happens "out there" this year, your family will be protected.

What you need to do in 2009

- Build a substantial savings account today so you will be okay if you are laid off.
- Do not—repeat, do not—go without health insurance.
- Shop for private health insurance if you are laid off; it is often less expensive than COBRA.
- Purchase an affordable term life insurance policy if anyone is dependent on your income.
- Make sure you have all your estate-planning documents in order.

Your 2009 Action Plan: Protecting Your Family and Yourself

SITUATION: You are worried you may lose your job in 2009.

ACTION: Prepare for it. As I write, the unemployment rate has already crept up from less than 5% in 2007 to 6.5% in October 2008. If we in fact fall into a hard landing, I would not be surprised to see unemployment rise to 8% or even 9%.

The best way to protect your family is to know that you will still be able to pay the bills while you look for a new job. Because of the weak economy, that could take longer than you may think. That is why it is imperative that you build an emergency savings account that can cover your family's living expenses for eight months. I know that is a lot, but you have got to start saving as much as you can right now. In "Action Plan: Spending," I review the steps you and your family can take to rein in your spending today so you have more money to put into a safe savings account.

And if you flew past the Action Plans for credit and real estate, I want to make sure you are up to speed on the fact that you may not be able to tap your credit card or a home equity line of credit to pay your family's bills in the event you are laid off. Lenders are not in the lending mood these days. I cannot be more emphatic: You must have savings set aside to be truly safe in 2009.

You also want to start your job hunt right now—while you still have your current job. Network like crazy, show up at industry conferences, and take a look at job postings in your field. If there is any specific skill mentioned that you are not up to speed on, get yourself schooled on it ASAP. In a slow economy, employers won't hire someone who meets 80% of their needs; they have such a large pool to choose from that they can find the person who meets 100% of their needs. Make sure that person is you.

SITUATION: You figure you will get by on unemployment benefits if you are laid off.

ACTION: You will still need to supplement that money with your own savings. The reality is that your maximum unemployment benefit typically will replace less than 50% of your lost wages. There is also a time limit to those payouts; 26 weeks is the standard amount of time you are eligible to collect unemployment. In harsh economic times, Congress can vote to extend the benefit period for an additional 13 weeks. (Unemployment is handled by your state, based on general standards set by federal law.)

To find out your state's rules, go to www.servicelocator.org and click on the "Find Unemployment Insurance Filing Assistance" link on the left side of the page.

SITUATION: You plan to use your credit card or HELOC to cover your expenses if you lose your job.

ACTION: You must have money set aside in a regular bank savings account or money market mutual fund in 2009. The lines of credit you have relied on in the past may not be available this year; without your own savings set aside, you could face a serious cash crunch if you are laid off and have no way to pay the bills.

Here's what you need to understand: Lenders are one step ahead of you. They, too, are worried that you will lose your job in 2009, and they are not fools. They know if that happens you will then use your credit card or HELOC to cover your bills, and because you don't have a job, that increases the likelihood that you won't be able to keep up with the payments on that borrowed money. That's very bad for their business, and let's just say they are extra sensitive right now given the bad shape they are already in. So, to head off this problem, lenders have been cutting back on what they allow customers to borrow. Credit card lines are being reduced, as are HELOCs.

If you haven't seen your credit lines change yet, don't think you can skate through because you have a sparking FICO score and a solid credit history. If you suddenly start to run up a balance on your credit card or tap a HELOC line you opened three years ago, that is going to set off warning bells for the lender, and you could very well see your credit lines disappear—just when you need them the most. The only safe alternative in 2009 is to have cash set aside in a savings account.

SITUATION: You plan to make early withdrawals from your 401(k) if you are laid off and can't pay your bills.

ACTION: Try as hard as you can not to touch your retirement savings. What seems like a reasonable action to help you get through problems today will devastate your long-term security. You need that money for retirement; spend it today and you will have less tomorrow. And don't tell me you will worry about that later, or you will boost your savings when you get another job. Even the best of intentions to make up for the withdrawals can run into harsh realities: Your next job may not pay enough to allow you to save to make up for your early withdrawal. (That said, if you feel you are out of options and need to raid your retirement funds to get by, please review my advice in "Action Plan: Retirement Investing" about how you may be able to take money out of your 401(k) without having to pay the typical 10% early withdrawal penalty.)

There is one important action I want you to take with your 401(k) if you are laid off in 2009: Roll over the money into an IRA at a brokerage or mutual fund company. As I explain in "Action Plan: Retirement Investing," rolling your money into an IRA gives you access to the best low-cost mutual funds and ETFs, rather than limiting yourself to the investment choices in your 401(k). And because of the steep market declines, if you qualify to roll over your money into a Roth IRA in 2009 you will get a great tax break.

SITUATION: You don't have money to set aside in savings.

ACTION: Get serious about finding ways to come up with real savings—right now. This is non-negotiable: You must build up a savings reserve. In "Action Plan: Spending," I explain how you and your family can (and must) adjust to the new realities of 2009 to find ways to reduce your expenses—or increase your income—so you have money to put toward important financial goals. And in 2009, there is nothing more important than building an emergency savings fund that can carry your family for eight months.

SITUATION: You dropped health insurance coverage through your employer in 2009 because it was too expensive and you are healthy.

ACTION: Get insurance now. If you can't get it from your employer, shop for your own policy. I don't care how healthy you are today. It's tomorrow I am worried about, and you and I both know a serious accident or sudden illness is always a possibility. Remember: Hope for the best, prepare for the worst. You need to understand that many of the families that end up filing for bankruptcy did so because they had unexpected medical bills that were impossible to pay off. Having health insurance reduces your financial burden if anyone in your family becomes severely ill or injured. Now, the truth is, insurance doesn't absolutely protect you from bankruptcy. The sad fact is that even people with insurance end up in bankruptcy because of high copays and costs that aren't covered. But the point is that insurance offers you some protection, whereas without insurance you have no protection.

I appreciate how expensive it is. Employers have been increasing charges to employees for their coverage; that can mean higher premiums, higher co-pays, or reductions in the scope of coverage. This is happening because health insurance costs keep rising at a rapid rate and companies are hard-pressed to shoulder the cost, and also because businesses feel the pressure to boost earnings (or minimize losses). Shifting more benefit costs onto employees helps the corporate bottom line.

Regardless of cost, you must have some insurance. If your old plan is too expensive, you should have shopped around for less expensive options within the plan. The reality is that because you turned down coverage during the open-enrollment period, typically in the fall, you may be shut out from restarting your coverage until the next enrollment period. (Certain exceptions apply for new employees and employees with life-changing events, such as a divorce or job change; check with your human resources department.) If that's the case, I am asking you to get short-term coverage through a private plan until you are eligible to get back on your company's plan.

SITUATION: You want to wait to see what options you may have if Washington passes health care reform in 2009.

ACTION: Don't wait for Washington to save you. You need protection right now. It could be months or years before any meaningful legislation is passed, assuming anything is passed. Moreover, it is unlikely that any sweeping reform would go into effect immediately. Typically, there is a transition period of many months. In the interim, you need insurance. You can always drop it if and when we have reform. That's one nice thing about health insurance: You pay your premium monthly, rather than annually. So you can drop the coverage whenever you want.

SITUATION: You don't know where to find affordable health insurance.

ACTION: Go to ehealthinsurance.com, the largest online resource for health insurance. If you prefer to work with an agent, the National Association of Health Underwriters (nahu.org) has an online search tool to give you leads on agents who help clients find individual health insurance policies. As you shop, realize that the group plan at your old job probably included a full menu of broad coverage—including mental health and maternity benefits, prescription drug coverage, and so on—that you may not need. Shop for a policy that provides only the specific coverage you need to keep your premium cost as low as possible.

SITUATION: You were laid off and can't afford the COBRA rate for your company's health insurance.

ACTION: Shop for less expensive health insurance. But do not—repeat, do not—go without health insurance. You can't afford to be uninsured. What if someone in your family becomes ill or is in a serious accident in 2009? Ehealthinsurance.com has created a Web site specifically for people who have been laid off; it includes a calculator to help you see what alternatives to COBRA might cost: www.ehealthinsurance.com/ehi/healthinsurance/cobra-learning-center.html.

SITUATION: You wonder whether you should keep the health insurance from your former employer or shop for a private plan.

ACTION: In many cases, a private plan will be less expensive than staying on your company plan. Here's what you need to know: Every employer with more than 20 employees that offers health insurance is required by the federal COBRA regulation to allow employees who've been laid off to stay on the company plan for 18 months, with one very big catch: The employee is responsible for 100% of the cost of the plan, as well as an extra 2% to cover administration costs. That is not just 100% of your normal premium when you were an employee, but 100% of the total cost, including what your employer used to pay on your behalf. So that can be a lot more than you were paying as an employee.

SITUATION: **You were let go and you have a preexisting health condition. You worry that you will not qualify for a private plan or it will be too expensive.**

ACTION: Stay on the company plan through COBRA, but get a private insurance plan for your family. Assuming your family is in good health, the cost of a private insurance plan for them will be less than continuing their coverage through COBRA.

At the same time, find a health insurance broker with extensive experience working with clients with preexisting conditions. (Go to nahu.org to find a list of agents in your area.) Different insurers have different policies; you want to work with someone who will shop around to locate a plan that may work for you. If you can't secure a private policy, you may have to opt for coverage offered through your state. This can often be very costly, so it is definitely to be used as a last resort.

You can find links to your state insurance department at naic.org (National Association of Insurance Commissioners).

SITUATION: You were told your state doesn't offer coverage to all residents.

ACTION: Stay on COBRA for as long as possible and lean on lawmakers for health care reform. I am sorry to say that there are indeed many states that do not have any last-resort coverage available for residents who can't qualify for an individual private policy. Just five states—Maine, Massachusetts, New Jersey, New York, and Vermont—have programs in place that offer guaranteed insurance at all times and to all residents. In Rhode Island, North Carolina, and Virginia (and in some instances Pennsylvania), you may be able to get last-resort coverage if you have been turned down for private policies. Contact your state health insurance commissioner's office to find out what's offered where you live; or look up your state's health insurance options on www.coverageforall.org.

SITUATION: You lost your job and the only new job you have been offered doesn't come with health benefits.

ACTION: Do not base your job search on health benefits. Take the job and shop for your own individual policy or continue on your old employer's plan through COBRA. But you need to choose COBRA coverage within 60 days of being notified you were COBRA-eligible; if more time has already passed, you have lost your right to stay on your old employer's plan.

SITUATION: You were laid off and want to go back to school so you can change careers.

ACTION: Get a job; school can wait. I am all for changing careers—hey, I spent my first seven years after college working as a waitress—but I am always suspicious when I hear someone tell me they want to go back to school right after they were laid off. It becomes this nice safety blanket to wrap yourself in, rather than dealing with a tough job market. But if you haven't really thought through what your new career is and you haven't figured out a financial plan for how you will pay for school, then it becomes a lousy idea. What are you going to live on while you go back to school? Don't think you can touch your emergency savings plan. That's for emergencies. Going back to school is not an emergency. It is a choice. Plan on taking out loans? Okay, but again, what are you going to live on while you are in school? Credit cards? That's never a good idea, and as I explain in "Action Plan: Credit," it may not even be possible in 2009.

A career change can be the best move you will ever make, but it requires careful planning. I say focus on getting another job right now, even if it's just for a year or so, while you carefully plan your new career and build up your savings so you can afford to go back to school.

SITUATION: You were laid off after 20 years with the same company. You are having a hard time finding a new job at the same salary and level of responsibility.

ACTION: Be realistic. What you made at your last job is somewhat irrelevant. What employers are willing to pay today for the job they have today is what really matters. For people who have spent a lot of time at one company, this is a tough concept to accept. But it is vitally important, especially when we can expect a tough job market in 2009.

People who have been with the same company for many years may have developed special skills particular to that company or industry, and they may have been well compensated for that expertise. But there is no guarantee your next employer needs those very skills or values them as much as your former employer did. These are not boom times; you can't set your price and then wait patiently for the right offer to come around. In tough times, you take the best offer available and appreciate that you have a job that allows you to support your family. If that means your family needs to get by on less income, well, that's just another reality to face in 2009. In "Action Plan: Spending," I have advice on how families can make more out of less.

SITUATION: You received a four-month severance package and plan on taking two months off to relax and regroup before beginning your job hunt.

ACTION: I wouldn't do it. Sure, take a few weeks to decompress and refresh. But given the slowdown in the economy, you need to start the job hunt sooner rather than later. It could very well take a lot longer than you expect.

SITUATION: You have life insurance through your employer. What happens to it if you are laid off?

ACTION: Whether you're laid off or not, I want you to get your own coverage. I have never recommended relying on employer-provided life insurance. If your employer provides coverage for free, chances are you are woefully uninsured; employer-provided life insurance is typically equal to one or two times your annual salary. I recommend 10 to 20 times to fully protect your family. Even if you buy extra insurance through your employer, it can often be more expensive than what you can get on your own; that's because you are paying a group rate based on all employees—young, old, healthy, not so healthy.

Another problem is that when you are laid off you eventually (within 18 months) need to convert to your own policy. And there is no guarantee the insurer who offered you group coverage will offer you an individual policy or one that is the least costly.

SITUATION: You haven't bought life insurance because you can't afford to.

ACTION: If there are people in your life who are dependent in any way on the income you earn, then you can't afford not to have life insurance. Seriously, what will happen to them if you die prematurely? Be it young kids, older parents who require financial assistance, or a sibling you help out—if you do not have sufficient assets your dependents can live off of, you need life insurance.

I think you will also be surprised by how remarkably affordable term life insurance is. A $1 million 20-year term policy for a healthy 45-year-old woman can cost less than $125 a month.

SITUATION: You're not sure if you should get term insurance or whole-life insurance.

ACTION: For the vast majority of us, term insurance is all that is needed.

As its name implies, term insurance is a policy for a specific period of time, the term. If you die during the term, your beneficiaries receive the death benefit (payout) from the insurer. And here's what you need to know: Chances are you have only a temporary need for life insurance. You need insurance while your kids are young and dependent on you; once they are adults, they will be financially independent. You need life insurance if you have yet to build up other assets (home equity, retirement investments) that will support your dependents when you die. Once you have those assets in place, it is less likely your surviving spouse or partner would need income from a life insurance policy in the event you pass away first.

Many insurance agents will tell you term is not enough. They will tell you that you want a permanent policy that never expires. Permanent policies come in a few different flavors: whole life, universal life, and variable life. I want to repeat: If your need for insurance is temporary—say, just until your youngest is through college—you absolutely do not need a permanent policy. And you will needlessly spend tens of thousands of dollars more for a permanent policy than a term policy.

SITUATION: You don't know how to shop for term insurance.

ACTION: You can shop online; selectquote.com and accuquote.com specialize in working with individuals who need term insurance. You will be asked to fill out a comprehensive worksheet of your income and assets as well as your expenses and debt. How much life insurance you need depends on those factors. If you want to be absolutely sure your family will be financially well off if you die prematurely, I would consider buying a policy with a death benefit equal to 20 times your family's annual income needs. Full disclosure: That is more than double what many insurance agents may recommend. You can indeed help your family tremendously with a smaller amount of coverage, but I am asking you to consider 20× for absolute peace of mind. If your death benefit is 20× your family's annual needs, they can take the payout and invest in conservative bonds (such as insured municipal bonds) and live off the principal amount. If your death benefit is smaller, they will eventually need to dip into the principal and it could sharply reduce how long the money lasts.

SITUATION: You have a term life insurance policy, but you're worried your insurer will go out of business.

ACTION: Know that your state insurance department will be looking out for you. The insurance department oversees a state guaranty association that provides coverage (up to the limits spelled out by state law) for policyholders of insurers licensed to do business in their state. In the case of life insurance, the guaranty association and state insurance commissioner will aim to have a healthy company take over the policies, so you will not see a change. You can find out how the guaranty system safety net operates in your state by visiting the National Organization of Life & Health Insurance Guaranty Associations' Web site: http://www.nolhga.com/policyholderinfo/main.cfm.

SITUATION: You can't sleep at night because you are so worried about what the world will look like for your children.

ACTION: Focus on what is in your control; make sure you have truly protected your family by having all essential estate-planning documents in place.

I know these are scary times, and it is sobering to wonder how long it will take for America and the global economy to work their way back to financial health. But I remain confident that with time we will get back on our feet. To invoke the analogy I made in the first chapter of this book, we are in the ICU right now, but with time we will make a full recovery.

What always amazes me is that often people who worry about the fate of our economy fail to protect their own family. I have to tell you, the bigger risk to your family is not what happens with GDP growth over the next two quarters; it is how well you have prepared your family in the event you become ill or die.

SITUATION: You aren't sure what estate-planning documents you need.

ACTION: You need a revocable living trust with an incapacity clause, as well as a will. Read that again. A will is not enough. I want you to also have a revocable living trust. And you need two durable powers of attorney—one for health care and one for finances. A power of attorney designates someone you trust to carry out your affairs in the event you become unable to handle matters on your own. Your health care power of attorney will be your "voice" in medical decisions if you are unable to speak for yourself, and the financial power of attorney can handle your bills and financial affairs. You also need an advance directive that spells out your wishes for the level of medical care you want should you become too ill to speak for yourself.

10

The Road Ahead

I began this book with the recognition that it is absolutely understandable for you to feel fear, anger, and confusion as you struggle with the repercussions of the global financial crisis.

However, I believe that the very severity of the crisis means that we will choose to make lasting changes that will put us on a path to a healthier and more vibrant future. Crises force us to take a clear-eyed view of what went wrong and compel us to make necessary adjustments to avoid the same pain and suffering again.

The period of reflection we are in right now has forced us to focus on a difficult reworking of our relationship with money. The era of living beyond our means is giving way to an age of living a more meaningful life based on financial honesty.

As painful as this transition period is, please

know that what awaits us is a very bright future. Our economy is suffering from a credit crisis, not a crisis of talent or drive. From the innovation that will continue to spill out of Silicon Valley to the reinvention now being discussed to transform our energy sources, I remain convinced that this is still a nation of unwavering discovery and achievement. Short term we have to survive the credit crisis and recession; long term we will prevail and we will thrive again.

Your job right now is to do the right thing when it comes to your money—to make a plan, to stick to it, to become a saver not a spender, to set a goal to live a debt-free life. I ask that you never forget the painful lessons that 2008 taught us. I ask you to remember these three things:

When it comes to money, if it sounds too good to be true, it is.

If you cannot afford it, do not buy it.

Always choose to do what's right, not what's easy.

My hope is that reading this book has given you an understanding that you are a huge part of the solution to your current problems. Despite the turmoil, despite the adversity, you have to recognize just how much is within your control. A secure financial future is in large part going to be a function of how willing you are to take action *today*. It won't appear out of thin air, it won't be legislated for you by Washington. It will grow out of the actions you take each and every day for the rest of your life.

Are you ready to make change happen in your own life? If you are, I hope this book becomes your guide. Here's to making your life, this precious time, the best it can be.

Suze Orman
November 19, 2008

About the Author

Suze Orman has been called "a force in the world of personal finance" and a "one-woman financial advice powerhouse" by *USA Today.* A two-time Emmy Award-winning television host, # 1 *New York Times* bestselling author, magazine and online columnist, writer/producer, and one of the top motivational speakers in the world today, Orman is undeniably America's most recognized expert on personal finance.

Orman has written six consecutive *New York Times* bestsellers and has written, co-produced, and hosted six PBS specials based on her books. She is the host of the award-winning *Suze Orman Show*, which airs on CNBC and XM and Sirius radio, and a contributing editor to *O, The Oprah Magazine.*

In 2008, Orman was named one of *Time* magazine's "Time 100," the world's most influential people, and was the recipient of the National Equality Award from the Human Rights Campaign. In 2009 she will receive an honorary doctor of humane letters degree from the University of Illinois at Urbana-Champaign

Orman, a CERTIFIED FINANCIAL PLANNER™ professional, directed the Suze Orman Financial Group from 1987 to 1997, served as Vice President-Investments for Prudential-Bache Securities from 1983 to 1987, and was an Account Executive at Merrill Lynch from 1980 to 1983. Prior to that, she worked as a waitress at the Buttercup Bakery in Berkeley, California, from 1973 to 1980.